Nursing and The Law

Second Edition

Edited by:

The Health Law Center
and

Charles J. Streiff, Esquire

Aspen Systems Corporation
Rockville, Maryland

Library of Congress Catalog Card Number: 74-32595
ISBN: 0-912862-04-1

Printed in United States of America.

CONTENTS

PART II. THE NURSE AND THE EMPLOYER

PART III. THE NURSE AND SOCIETY

INTRODUCTION

THE BASIC AIM OF THIS BOOK IS TO AID THE PRACTICING NURSE IN THOSE MATTERS
where a nurse's functions and responsibilities are addressed by the Law.
Nursing and the Law recognizes that nurses are committed to the mission
of selflessly healing and aiding suffering humanity; however, this general
mission sometimes presents inherent conflicts where basic societal and individual rights must be accorded every person, whether in or outside the
health delivery system.

A nurse touches, not only the lives of patients on a day-to-day basis, but
also some very important aspects of society's continuing development. Advances in technology, which change what is possible, and evolutions in
philosophy, which change what is desirable, are recognized in the Law by
processes considerably slower than the forces acting on either technology or
philosophy. There exists, more often than not, a gap between the
perceived needs of society and help in fulfilling those needs, which Law is
able to provide. One favorable aspect of this delay is that a fairly strong
consensus can be accumulated to accompany changes in the Law; this
helps to increase both understanding and acceptance.

The Law should not be feared; and recognizing that understanding can
dispel fear, the Health Law Center has prepared *Nursing and the Law*.
Conflicts or contradictions which seem to exist between the nurse's con-
ceded overall mission and limits and constraints on day-to-day functions
reflect certain general and certain specific concepts in Law. Once these
basic viewpoints are recognized, the nurse will, with some confidence, be
able to possibly assist with changes in process, while, more importantly,
providing the best practice possible.

Nursing and the Law, though written by lawyers, directs itself not to the
problems faced by lawyers in solving nurses' legal problems, but rather to
the impact the Law has on Nursing. *Nursing and the Law,* is clarifying the
relationships and responsibilities enunciated by the Law, provides the

nurse with general, though reasonable, criteria. These criteria apply not only to registered nurses working in an institutional setting, but also to nurses in private offices, special duty nurses, practical nurses, student nurses and even hospital volunteers and aides.

While *Nursing and the Law* is a work which has its roots in the information resources of Aspen's Health Law Center, special recognition is accorded Charles J. Streiff, J.D., who provided that essential awareness and scrutiny which only an interested and skilled intellect can offer, and without which this book may never have been written.

Gerald Seifert, Director
The Health Law Center
Rockville, Maryland
March, 1975

PART I

THE NURSE AND HER PATIENTS

PRINCIPLES
OF
NURSING LIABILITY

PROFESSIONAL NURSES, LIKE EVERYONE ELSE, ARE LIABLE FOR ANY HARM THAT results from personally negligent acts. Nurses are held to a standard of care expected of reasonably competent nurses. The fact that they provide services to patients in a hospital as employees of the hospital does not relieve the nurses of personal legal responsibility to the patients in their care.

Section 1
DEFINITION OF MALPRACTICE
AND NEGLIGENCE

Malpractice is the term for negligence or carelessness of professional personnel. To determine what is and what is not careless, the law has developed a measuring scale called the standard of care. Usually, the standard of care is determined by deciding what a reasonably prudent person acting under similar circumstances would do. A jury makes this determination.

This reasonably prudent person is a legal fiction—in other words, a hypothetical average person with average skills and training in the relevant field and with a hypothetically average amount of judgment and good sense. What this person would do is the yardstick for measuring what others should do in similar circumstances. Once the determination is made as to what the reasonably prudent person would have done, the actual performance of the person who is charged with negligence is measured against that standard of care.

If the action of the person charged (the defendant) meets or surpasses the standard, there has been no negligence or carelessness, just an unavoidable occurrence. But if the defendant's actions fail to meet the standard, then there has been negligence, and the jury must make two determinations: First, was it foreseeable that harm would follow the failure to meet the standard of care? Second, was the carelessness or negligence the proximate or immediate cause of the harm or injury to the plaintiff? A nurse who fails to meet the standard of care will be liable for negligence if that failure results in harm to another.

The four elements of negligence are: (1) a standard of due care under the circumstances; (2) a failure to meet the standard of due care; (3) the foreseeability of harm resulting from failure to meet the standard; and (4) the fact that the breach of this standard proximately causes the injury to the plaintiff.

A nurse may be negligent and still not incur liability if no injury results to another person. The term "injury" includes more than mere physical harm. In some states it may include mental anguish and other invasions of rights and privileges. For example, a wife whose husband has been hospitalized as a result of a third person's negligence may sue that third person for loss of marital services.

To prove what the reasonably prudent nurse would do, the courts utilize the services of an expert witness, a person trained in nursing or medicine who can testify to what the professional standard of care is in the same or similar communities. This testimony is necessary because the jury is not trained or qualified to determine what the reasonably prudent nurse's standard of care would be under the circumstances. Essentially, the expert testifies to aid the judge and the jury, by providing a measure by which the actual conduct of the nurse can be properly assessed.

In the performance of professional duties, every nurse is required to exercise reasonable care so that no harm or injury comes to any patients. The law measures the reasonableness of the care by the performance of other nurses in the community. Thus the standard of care for nurses is that degree of care ordinarily exercised by nurses of similar training and experience in the same or similar localities.

Some courts have moved away from the community standard of care and have applied what might be called a national standard. In this situation, the expert witness testifies as to what any reasonably prudent nurse anywhere would have done. The theory is that the standard of care should not vary according to the locale where the individual receives care.

The accompanying guidelines on negligence summarize the concepts of negligence and malpractice and the standard of care to be met in a particular situation. (See chart on page 5.)

Section 2

THE STANDARD OF CARE

NURSES

A professional nurse, in providing care to patients, is held to the prevailing standard of care. Thus, when injury has been suffered by a patient,

GUIDELINES ON NEGLIGENCE PROFESSIONAL NEGLIGENCE IS MALPRACTICE		
Elements of liability	Explanation	Example – Giving medications
1. Duty to use due care (defined by the standard of care)	The care which should be given under the circumstances (what the reasonably prudent nurse would have done)	A nurse should give medications: ● accurately and ● completely and ● on time
2. Failure to meet standard of care (breach of duty)	Not giving the care which should be given under the circumstances	A nurse fails to give medications: ● accurately or ● completely or ● on time
3. Foreseeability of harm	Knowledge that not meeting the standard of care will cause harm to the patient	Giving the wrong medication or the wrong dosage or not on schedule will probably cause harm to the patient
4. Failure to meet standard of care (breach) *causes* injury	Patient is harmed because proper care is not given	Wrong medication causes patient to have a convulsion
5. Injury	Actual harm results to patient	Convulsion or other serious complication

in order to hold the nurse liable for negligence it must be shown that the nurse failed to meet the standard. The fact that injury is suffered, without proof that the nurse deviated from the practice of competent members of the nursing profession, is not sufficient for imposing liability upon the nurse.

Whether a nurse adhered to a standard of care generally practiced by the nursing profession in the community was a question raised in *Norton v. Argonaut Insurance Co.,* [144 So. 2d 249 (La. Ct. App. 1902)]. That case involved the entry of an erroneous or ambiguous order upon a patient's chart by the attending physician and focused on the responsibility of a nurse to obtain clarification of the medication order.

The nurse in the *Norton* case, familiar only with the injectable form of the medication and unaware of the elixir form which was far less potent, believed the order to be incorrect. She asked two physicians present in the ward whether she should give the medication as ordered by the attending physician. The physicians did not interpret the order in the way that the nurse did and therefore did not share her concern. They told her to follow the attending physician's instructions. The nurse did not contact the attending physician but instead administered the medication according to her understanding of the order. The patient died as a result of the administration of the medication in the injectable form rather than the elixir form.

The court found that the nurse had been negligent in failing to contact the attending physician before she gave the medication. In its opinion the court specifically discussed the requisite standard of care applicable to the nurse. Given the facts of the case, this standard required that the nurse call the prescribing physician when in doubt about an order for medication—a standard that the court considered most reasonable and prudent. In its opinion the court stated that the same rules which govern the duties and liabilities of physicians in the performance of professional services to their patients applied to nurses as well.

This articulation of the standard of care applicable to nurses was followed by the same court in *Thompson v. Brent,* [245 So. 2d 751 (La. Ct. App. 1971)]. In this case the medical assistant of the defendant physician removed a cast from the plaintiff's arm with an electrically powered saw known as a Stryker saw. While sawing through the cast, the assistant cut the plaintiff's arm, thereby causing a residual scar almost the length of the cast and the width of the saw blade. Following the *Norton* case, the court held that, in determining whether the physician's assistant was negligent in the use of the saw, it was necessary to consider the degree of care which would have been demanded of the physician had he removed the cast himself. Applying this standard, the court found the assistant's conduct negligent and the physician liable for the negligence under the doctrine of *respondeat superior.*

It may well be that the statement of the court in the *Norton* decision meant no more than that, as physicians are measured against the standard of competent medical performance, so nurses are measured against the standard of competent nursing performance. However, even with this latter interpretation, a basis for liability could be found in the *Thompson* case.

Underlying much of the litigation concerned with the liability of nurses for negligence is the determination of what constitutes the standard of good nursing practice. In *Mundt v. Alta Bates Hospital,* [35 Cal. Rptr. 848, 223 Cal. App. 2d 413 (1963)], a *California* court was faced with conflicting testimony concerning a nurse's responsibilities after observing increasing swelling and redness in the area of a "cut-down." The patient had been seriously injured as the result of excessive infiltration from an intravenous infusion over a long period of time. The attending physician testified that a nurse who observes swelling or redness at the site of a cut-down must either notify the attending physician or turn off the intravenous infusion. He further testified that, had the nurse stopped the flow of the intravenous solution when the swelling reached a critical point, serious injury would have been averted. There was other testimony from nurses to the effect that a nurse who observes swelling or other danger signs in the area of a cut-down should notify the attending physician; but, without an order from the physician, the nurse could not cut off the flow of the intravenous solution. These standards differed on the issue of whether a nurse should stop the flow of the solution without an order, and the court did not decide which standard should be applied to determine whether the nurse was negligent. The case was sent back for a new trial, and the court recognized that selecting the standard to be applied would be left for the jury to decide. If the standard allowing a nurse to halt an intravenous infusion without an order were applied, it would be much more likely that the nurse who failed to take such action would be held negligent. Of course, if the other standard were accepted by the jury and applied, the nurse probably would not be held liable.

Although sometimes, as in the *Mundt* case, there may be inconsistent evidence of the standard of nursing practice by competent nurses, often there is little difficulty in determining the standard against which the allegedly negligent nurse is to be measured. Thus in *Weinstein v. Prostkoff*, [23 Misc. 2d 376, N.Y.S. 2d. 310 (1959)] the nurse was held liable for negligence in the administration of an anesthetic. Information had not been obtained as to whether the patient had partaken of food within a reasonably short time before nitrous oxide was administered, and the nurse did not check the mask, as is customary, to watch for signs that gastric contents were coming up. The patient was found to have been asphyxiated because the breathing passages were blocked with vomitous material.

When a nurse failed to read all the entries in the patient's record pertaining to the administration of a particular medication, such failure was found to be negligence. The case of *Larrimore v. Homeopathic Hospital Association,* [54 Del. 449, 181 A.2d 573 (1962)] concerned a female patient who had been receiving a drug by injection over a period of time. The physician wrote an order on the patient's order sheet changing the mode of administration from injection to oral administration.

When the nurse on the unit, who had been off duty for several days, was preparing to give the medication to the patient by injection, the patient objected and referred the nurse to the physician's new order. The nurse, however, told the patient she was mistaken and gave the medication by injection. Perhaps the nurse had not reviewed the order sheet after being told by the patient that the medication was to be given orally, or perhaps the nurse did so in a negligent manner and did not notice the physician's entry. Either way, the nurse's conduct was held to be negligent. The court went on to say that the jury could find the nurse negligent by applying ordinary common sense to establish the applicable standard of care.

Two Canadian cases demonstrate how the standard of care is applied in similar situations. Both involve nurses who left their posts to take coffee breaks. In one case the nurse was not found negligent and in the other case the nurse was found negligent. In *Child v. Vancouver General Hospital*, [71 W.W.R. 656 (1969)], the nurse left for a coffee break after the physician in charge had seen the patient and, as he later testified, the patient appeared "much improved." In deciding that the nurse was not negligent to leave such a patient unattended, the court emphasized that the question of liability should be determined in the light of the circumstances as they existed at the time. When the nurse left the patient, it was not foreseeable that an increased risk to the patient would be created.

However, in *Laidlaw v. Lions Gate Hospital*, [70 W.W.R. 727 (1969)], the court held that the nurse who left on a coffee break and the supervisor who allowed the nurse to leave might reasonably have anticipated needs for nursing care that could not be met during the nurse's absence. When the nurse left there were two patients in the recovery room with only one nurse to attend to them. Within a very brief time three other patients arrived, including the plaintiff, Mrs. Laidlaw; this meant there were now five paitents and only one nurse in the recovery room. Because the one nurse did not have sufficient time to minister properly to Mrs. Laidlaw, she suffered extensive, permanent brain damage as the result of insufficient oxygen while still under the anesthetic after surgery.

A nursing supervisor testified at the trial that there usually were two nurses present in the recovery room and that the nurses were expected to take their coffee breaks before any patients arrived. There was also testimony that the nurses on duty in the recovery room knew the operating schedule and should have anticipated the need for both to be present to meet the needs of patients who would be arriving at the unit. The court found that the nurse who took the coffee break and the supervisor who authorized the nurse's absence were negligent in leaving the recovery room with only one nurse in attendance.

Evidence of the standard of care applicable to nursing activities may also be found in regulations of a state governmental agency or of the federal government, as well as in the standards of the Joint Commission on Accreditation of Hospitals. The personnel of a hospital subject to such regulations or standards are responsible for meeting that standard of care prescribed; failure of a nurse to do so provides a basis for finding the nurse liable for negligence.

Changes in the standard of care for nurses reflect new kinds of duties which are being imposed upon the practice of nursing by statutes, regulations, hospital rules, and court cases. These duties include not only those directly related to nursing techniques and procedures but also duties affecting the way in which nurses work with others in the hospital. In the *Illinois* case, *Darling v. Charleston Community Memorial Hospital*, [33 Ill. 2d 326, 211 N.E. 2d 253 (1965)], a minor sued a hospital and a physician for allegedly negligent medical and hospital treatment which necessitated the amputation of his right leg below the knee. A judgment in favor of the plaintiff was affirmed by the Supreme Court of *Illinois*.

On November 5, 1960, the 18-year-old plaintiff in the *Darling* case broke his leg while playing in a college football game. He was taken to the hospital's emergency room and treated by the physician who was on emergency call that day. With the assistance of hospital personnel, the doctor applied traction and placed the leg in a plaster cast. A heat cradle was applied to dry the cast. Not long after the cast was applied the plaintiff complained of great pain in his toes, which protruded from the cast. The toes became swollen and dark, eventually they became cold and insensitive. On the evening of November 6, the physician "notched" the cast around the toes and on the afternoon of the following day he cut the cast approximately three inches above the foot. On November 8, he split the sides of the cast with a Stryker saw. The plaintiff's leg was cut on both sides while the cast was being removed. Blood and other seepage were observed by the nurses and others, and a great stench filled the room.

The plaintiff remained in the hospital until November 19, when he was transferred to a hospital in St. Louis and placed under the care of an orthopedic specialist. The specialist found that the fractured leg contained a considerable amount of dead tissue. In his opinion this resulted from interference with blood circulation when the leg swelled or hemorrhaged against the cast. The specialist performed several operations in a futile attempt to save the leg, but ultimately it had to be amputated eight inches below the knee.

The plaintiff contended that in this case, it was the duty of the nurses to watch the protruding toes constantly for color, temperature, and movement, as well as to check circulation every 10 to 20 minutes. According to the evidence in the case, these things were done only a few times a day. The plaintiff also argued that the hospital was negligent in failing to have, for bedside care of all patients at all times, a sufficient number of trained nurses capable of recognizing the progressive gangrenous condition of the plaintiff's right leg and of bringing it to the attention of the hospital administration and the medical staff.

The court held that on the basis of the evidence, it could reasonably conclude that the nurses did not test for circulation in the leg as frequently as necessary, whereas skilled nurses would have promptly recognized the conditions that signal a dangerous impairment of circulation and would have known that the condition would become irreversible in a matter of hours. It was the duty of the nurses to inform the attending physician of the prevailing conditions and, if the physician failed to act, to advise the hospital authorities so that appropriate action could have been taken.

The *Darling* case was not the first instance of a court's finding it a nurse's duty to bring appropriate matters to the attention of the physicians in charge of a case or to alert the hospital authorities. In *Goff v. Doctors General Hospital,* [166 Cal. App. 2d 314, 333 P.2d 29(1958)], the court held that nurses who attended a mother, and who knew she was bleeding excessively, were negligent in failing to report the circumstances so that prompt and adequate measures could be taken to safeguard her life.

Nursing procedures become more complicated; nurses work in closer connection with physicians in the performance of medical and surgical procedures; and it has recently been recognized as a duty of nurses to bring appropriate matters before the proper authorities. Failure to exercise that duty will lead to liability not only of the nurses but also of the hospital under the doctrine of *respondeat superior*. However, court recognition of this duty has not gone as far as providing guidance to nurses on the proper manner of fulfilling this duty. Thus in order to live up to this duty, nurses will have to be aware of the many problems involved and will also have to make careful decisions about when to report and when not to report to their superiors.

STUDENT NURSES

As part of their educational program, student nurses are entrusted with the responsibility of providing certain kinds of nursing care to patients. When liability is being assessed, the student nurse serving at the hospital in a patient care unit is considered an employee of the hospital. This is true even if the student is on affiliation and is not a student of the hospital's school of nursing. The nursing student will be personally liable for negligence if injury results, and the hospital will also be liable under the doctrine of *respondeat superior* for any harm suffered.

Although this may seem a harsh rule at first, a student nurse is held to the standard of a competent professional nurse when performing nursing duties. In several decisions, the courts have taken the position that anyone who performs duties customarily performed by professional nurses is held to the standards of professional nurses. Every patient has the right to expect competent nursing services, even if the care is provided by students as part of their clinical experience. From the patient's point of view, it would be unfair to deprive him of compensation for an injury because the hospital has undertaken to utilize students to provide nursing care.

What if the student nurse's negligence occurs while performing a task the student was not yet capable of performing in a manner consistent with the standard of competent professional nurses? In this situation the supervisor, whether a designated clinical instructor or the nurse in charge of the unit where the student is working, the supervisor can be found to have deviated from the standard of competent nursing practice applicable to a supervisor and can be held liable.

Until it is clearly demonstrated that student nurses are competent to render nursing services without increasing the risks of injury to patients, there must be more supervision than is ordinarily provided for professional nurses.

NURSING SUPERVISORS

The legal issues arising from the nurses' supervisory responsibilities affect both supervisory nurses and staff nurses who have no supervisory titles but nevertheless direct personnel in the performance of their duties. A nurse with supervisory responsibility is not liable merely because one of the persons to whom duties have been assigned or delegated is negligent and thereby causes harm to a patient. The supervisor is liable only for negligence in carrying out supervisory duties. The supervisor's liability should be clearly distinguished from the liability of the employer—the hospital—for negligence under the doctrine of *respondeat superior*. The nurse with supervisory responsibilities is not the employer; the hospital is the employer and the supervising nurse is another hospital employee who has administrative responsibility for the performance of subordinate personnel.

Thus if a nursing supervisor assigns a task to an individual who the supervisor knows or should have known is not competent to perform the particular task, and if a patient suffers injury because of incompetent performance of the task, the supervisor can be held personally liable for negligence as a supervisor. The hospital will be liable, under the doctrine of *respondeat superior,* as the employer of both the supervisor and the individual who performed the task in a negligent fashion. The supervisor is not relieved of personal liability even though the hospital is liable under *respondeat superior.*

In determining whether a nurse with supervisory responsibilities has been negligent, the nurse is measured against the standard of care of a competent and prudent nurse in the performance of supervisory duties. If charting a patient's fluid intake were assigned to a nurse's aide who had not been instructed in performing this task, and if such an assignment is not usually made until the supervisor personally ascertains whether the aide knows how to chart fluids satisfactorily, this departure from the standard of care would constitute a basis for imposing liability for negligence if a patient were harmed as a result.

A supervisor may ordinarily rely upon the fact that a subordinate is licensed or certified as an indication of the subordinate's capabilities in performing tasks within the ambit of the license or certificate. But where the individual's past actions have led the supervisor to believe that the person is likely to perform a task in an unsatisfactory manner, assigning the task to the person can lead to liability for negligence because the risk of harm to the patient is increased.

Section 3

DEFENSES

CONTRIBUTORY NEGLIGENCE

Once the plaintiff has established that a defendant has been negligent, the defendant may raise defenses to the claim for damages. The most common defense in a negligence action is contributory negligence, and, when established, constitutes a complete barrier to the plaintiff's damage claim.

When contributory negligence is raised, the defendant claims the conduct of the injured person to be below the standard of care a reasonably prudent man would exercise for his own safety. The two elements of contributory negligence are: (1) that the plaintiff's conduct is below the required standard of care; and (2) that there is a connection between the plaintiff's careless conduct and his injury. Thus, the defendant contends that the plaintiff contributed to the plaintiff's injury.

The rationale for contributory negligence is based on the principle that everyone must be both careful and responsible for his acts. Therefore, the plaintiff is required to conform to the same broad standard of conduct, that of the reasonable man of ordinary prudence under like circumstances, and the plaintiff's negligence will be determined and governed by the same tests and rules as the negligence of the defendant.

Contributory negligence is a defense to negligence *only*. It is not a defense if the defendant's conduct actually was intended to inflict harm upon the plaintiff such as, an intentional wrong of battery or false imprisonment.

ASSUMPTION OF RISK

The second most commonly used defense is assumption of risk. This defense simply means that the plaintiff has expressly given consent in advance, relieving the defendant of an obligation of conduct toward the plaintiff and taking the chances of injury from a known risk arising from the defendant's conduct. For example, a private duty nurse who agreed to care for a patie. . with a communicable disease, and who contracted the disease, would not be entitled to sue the former patient for loss of earnings. In taking the job, the nurse agreed to assume the risk of infection and thereby released the patient from all legal obligations.

In this case, if the nurse were to bring suit the patient could invoke the doctrine of assumption of risk as a defense. This is because the nurse's conduct must meet the two requirements necessary for the defense: first, that the plaintiff must know and understand the risk that is being incurred; and second, that the choice to incur the risk must be entirely free and voluntary.

COMPARATIVE NEGLIGENCE

Comparative negligence is recognized in only a few states. This doctrine relieves the plaintiff of the hardship of losing an entire claim when the defendant has entered a plea of contributory negligence. In many cases of negligence, there has been carelessness on the part of both parties. If the plaintiff is guilty of minor carelessness, whereas the defendant has been more grossly careless, forcing the plaintiff to lose the entire claim is considered too harsh a result in jurisdictions that recognize comparative negligence.

The doctrine provides that the degree of negligence or carelessness of each party be established by the finder of fact, and each be responsible for the appropriate proportion of the injuries. For example, where the plaintiff suffers injuries of $10,000 from an accident, and the plaintiff is found 20 percent negligent and the defendant 80 percent, the defendant would be required to pay $8,000 to the plaintiff. Thus with comparative negligence the plaintiff can collect for 80 percent of the injuries, whereas an application of contributory negligence would deprive the plaintiff of any money judgment.

STATUTE OF LIMITATIONS

Whether a suit for personal injury can be brought against a nurse often depends upon whether the suit has commenced within a time specified by the applicable statute of limitations. The statutory period begins when an injury occurs, although in some cases, usually involving foreign objects left in the body during surgery, the statutory period commences when the injured person discovers or should have discovered the injury.

There are many technical rules associated with statutes of limitations. Statutes in each state prescribe that malpractice suits and other personal injury suits must be brought within fixed periods of time, but court decisions and specific statutes in many states have extended the limitation periods substantially. For example, the fact that the injured person is a minor or is otherwise under a legal disability may, under the laws of many states, extend the period within which an action for injury may be brought.

CONSENT TO MEDICAL
AND
SURGICAL PROCEDURES

BEFORE ANY MEDICAL OR SURGICAL PROCEDURE CAN BE PERFORMED ON A PATIENT, even a procedure involving the simple movement of a patient's limb, the consent must be obtained from the patient or from someone authorized to consent on the patient's behalf. The reason for this is that the intentional touching of another without authorization to do so is a legal wrong called a battery. In a case of emergency the consent requirement does not apply.

Not every touching results in liability. When a person voluntarily enters a situation which a reasonable man would anticipate a touching, consent is implied. Thus consent is not required for the normal, routine touchings and bumpings that occur in life. But the law does require consent for the intentional touchings which occur in health care situations.

The question of liability for performing a medical or surgical procedure without the patient's consent is separate and distinct from any question of negligence or malpractice in performing the procedure. Liability may be imposed for a nonconsensual touching of the patient even if the procedure improved the patient's health.

Section 1

NATURE OF CONSENT

Consent is an authorization, by the patient or a person authorized by law to consent on the patient's behalf, that changes a touching from nonconsensual to consensual. Although most consent cases involve physicians, the principles of law concerning the nature of consent are equally applicable to hospitals and to nurses. In many cases it is the nurse who actually procures the consent.

A patient has a right to be secure in his person from any touching, and is free to reject treatment which medical advisers deem necessary. Therefore, before treatment is begun the patient's consent to treatment is needed,

15

along with substantial proof of that consent, so as to guard against liability because of an allegedly unlawful touching of the patient.

An authorization from the patient without a full understanding of what is being consented to is not effective consent. The patient must be given sufficient information to exercise freedom of choice. In other words, each patient has the right to make an intelligent choice from among the various courses of treatment possible as well as the right to refuse or reject a specific course of treatment. State courts are in wide disagreement as to the proper test for determining whether the information furnished to the patient was enough to provide a basis for effective consent. In recent court cases, two basic tests to determine the adequacy of disclosure have emerged.

The first, an objective test, requires the physician to provide as much information about a contemplated procedure as is ordinarily provided by other physicians in the community. This test was used in a *Wyoming* case, *Govin v. Hunter,* [374 P. 2d 421 (Wyo. 1962)]. According to the patient, the surgeon should have advised her that multiple incisions would be necessary in a vein stripping procedure and that scars and disfigurement of her leg would result. The court recognized that in some circumstances a physician has a duty to reveal any serious risks involved in a contemplated procedure, and it stated that the manner in which a physician chooses to discharge this duty is primarily a matter of medical judgment. The court denied the patient's claim because no proof was presented that the patient's physician departed from the practice of other competent physicians in informing patients about this procedure. In saying the proper standard was the practice of other competent physicians performing the same procedure, the court utilized an objective test. Thus the patient had the burden of proving that the physician departed from the standard practice. Because the patient failed to do this, she lost her case.

The second test, a subjective test, relies upon the patient's understanding of the physician's explanation of risks and probable consequences of the procedure. Thus a physician may be held liable if a jury finds that the information given the patient was not enough for informed consent. An example of this test is the *Florida* case, *Russell v. Harwick,* [166 So. 2d 904 (Fla. 1964)]. The patient had signed a consent form authorizing the physician to perform any operation he deemed advisable to repair her fractured hip. But the patient asserted that, had she been better informed about the procedure that was going to be used, she would not have authorized it and would instead have sought an orthpedic consultation. Expert testimony at the trial indicated that, in electing to remove the head of the femur and replace it with a metallic prosthesis, the physician had used the most satisfactory and most successful method of treating such a fracture. However, the patient had not been told that the leg would be shorter. The jury found the physician liable for malpractice, and the verdict was upheld by a higher court on the ground that the patient had a right to know the likely consequences of the contemplated treatment before deciding whether to give consent. It should be noted that the procedure itself was performed with care and was successful by medical standards.

Several recent cases indicate that the subjective test may evolve into a "reasonable man" standard to be applied by the judge or jury as the finder of facts. In *Canterbury v. Spence,* [464 F. 2d 772 (D.C. Cir. 1972)], the *District of Columbia* Circuit Court of Appeals said that whether the physician's disclosure was reasonable depends on what the physician knows or should know to be the patient's needs for information. Whether any danger in the proposed treatment must be disclosed depends upon whether it could be material to the patient's decision to accept or reject such treatment. The court explained that a risk is material when a reasonable person would be likely to attach significance to the risk in making the decision for or against treatment.

When a physician informs a competent adult patient that an operation is necessary, and the patient assents, an express consent has been obtained. Consent can also be implied, even though there is no explicit oral or written expression of consent. For example, a patient may voluntarily submit to a procedure; this constitutes implied consent, even without any explicit spoken or written expression of consent. In the *Massachusetts* case, *O'Brien v. Cunard S.S. Co.,* [154 Mass. 272, 28 N.E. 266 (1891)], a ship's passenger who joined a line of people receiving injections was held to have implied his consent to a vaccination. The rationale for this decision is that an individual who observes a line of people and notices that injections are being administered to those at the head of the line should expect that if he joins and remains in the line, he will receive an injection. Therefore, the voluntary act of entering the line, along with the opportunity to see what was taking place at the head of the line, was accepted by the jury as a manifestation of consent to the injection. The *O'Brien* case contains all the elements necessary to imply consent from a voluntary act: The procedure was a simple vaccination; the proceedings were at all times visible; and the plaintiff was free to withdraw up to the instant of the injection.

Voluntary submission itself does not always imply consent. *Woods v. Brumlop,* [71 N.M. 221, 377 P. 2d 520 (1962)], was the case of a patient who sustained injuries as the result of electroshock treatment. Although the patient had voluntary submitted to the treatment, she contended that her physician's failure to provide her with sufficient facts about the procedure rendered ineffective any consent implied from the voluntary submission. The court found that the voluntary submission patient was in the right. Thus, voluntary submission constitutes implied consent only if the patient is fully informed and apparently understands the nature and seriousness of the procedure—in other words, if actions and words, taken together, would cause a reasonable man to believe the patient was consenting to the procedure.

Whether the patient's consent can be implied is a frequent question when the condition of the patient requires some deviation from the procedure which was selected by the surgeon and discussed with the patient. If a patient expressly prohibits a specific medical or surgical procedure, consent to the procedure cannot be implied. The same consent rule applies if a patient expressly prohibits a particular extension of a procedure, even though the patient has voluntarily submitted to the original procedure. However, if a patient is apprised of the nature of the contemplated extension and its possible risks and results, the authorization of the extension is effective.

Section 2

HOSPITAL LIABILITY FOR
FAILURE TO OBTAIN CONSENT

The hospital may be liable if a medical or surgical procedure is performed without the patient's consent. This liablity is based on either of two theories: (1) the duty of the hospital to protect patients against injuries inflicted by third persons; or (2) the doctrine of *respondeat superior*. It is the hospital's duty to protect the patient when it has or should have knowledge of the patient's objections to the medical or surgical procedure and when the patient is legally or physically incapable of consent.

In *Fiorentino v. Wenger,* [280 N.Y.S. 2d 373, 223 N.E. 2d 46 (1967)], the plaintiff claimed that the hospital was liable because it failed to ensure adequate disclosure of the facts before its operating facilities were used. The patient, a minor, died of a hemorrhage subsequent to a novel surgical procedure designed to support the spine in a straight position. The surgical procedure was developed by the defendant surgeon, and he was the only one in the United States to use it. The court held that the hospital was not liable and did not have to verify whether an informed consent had been obtained. The court said the hospital did not need to intervene between the physician and the patient unless it knew or should have known that there had not been an informed consent or unless the performance of the procedure itself would constitute malpractice.

Under the doctrine of *respondeat superior* the hospital is liable for any battery by its employees which occurs within the scope of employment. The doctrine provides that the hospital will be held legally responsible for any wrongs of its employees while they are performing their duties. Rendering medical or surgical treatment to a patient without his consent is clearly a battery, and if performed by hospital personnel, the institution would be liable. Thus a nurse performing an act upon a patient to which the patient has not consented may create liability for the hospital. In these circumstances, the nurse may also be liable for battery.

Section 3
PROOF OF CONSENT

A written consent has one purpose only: to provide visible proof of consent. An oral consent, if proved, is just as binding as a written one, for there is no legal requirement that the patient's consent be in writing. However, an oral consent may be difficult to prove in court. A valid written consent must include these elements: It must be signed; it must show that the procedure was the one consented to; and it must show that the person consenting understood the nature of the procedure, the risks involved, and the probable consequences.

Many physicians and hospitals have relied on consent forms worded in such general terms that they permit the physician to perform any medical or surgical procedure believed to be in the patient's best interests. This kind of form is usually signed by the patient at the time of admission, but it does not constitute valid consent. There is little difference between a surgical patient who signed no authorization and one who signed a form consenting to whatever surgery the physician deems advisable. In both situations, testimony would be necessary to establish the extent of the patient's actual knowledge and understanding. It is possible for the patient, after treatment, to claim a lack of advance knowledge about the nature of the physician's treatment. And it is possible that a jury will believe the patient and impose liability upon the physician or the hospital or both.

The most satisfactory way to prove that the patient has consented to medical or surgical treatment is to use two integrated consent forms. An admission consent form should be signed when the patient is admitted to the hospital. This records the patient's consent to routine hospital services, diagnostic procedures, and medical treatment. [☞ For an explanation of admission consent form, see Appendix A.] A signed special consent form should be obtained before every medical or surgical treatment except the aforementioned routine activities. [☞ For an explanation of a special consent form, see Appendix B.]

Section 4
WHO MUST CONSENT

Consent of the patient is ordinarily required before treatment. However, when the patient is either physically unable or legally incompetent to consent, and no emergency exists, consent must be obtained from a person who is empowered to consent on the patient's behalf. The person who gives consent for treatment of another must have enough information to make an intelligent judgment, and the physician must disclose risks involved in the procedure.

CONSENT OF MINORS

When a medical or surgical procedure is to be performed upon a minor, the question arises whether the minor's consent alone is sufficient and, if not, from whom consent must be obtained.

When faced with this issue the courts have used as a point of reference the requirement of an adult's assent in order to make a minor's obligation binding in commercial matters. And the obligation is binding on the responsible parent, not on the minor. The courts have held that, as a general proposition, the consent of a minor to medical or surgical treatment is ineffective, and the physician must secure the consent of the minor's parent or someone standing *in loco parentis,* or must risk liability.

However, a number of courts have held the consent of a minor sufficient authorization for treatment in certain situations. In any specific case a court's determination that the consent of a minor is effective and parental consent unnecessary will depend upon factors such as the minor's age, maturity, marital status, and emancipation as well as on certain public policy considerations. An example of this more liberal view is the *Michigan* case of *Bishop v. Shurly,* [237 Mich. 76, 211 N.W. 75 (1926)]. The patient's mother contracted with the defendant doctor for the removal of her 19-year-old son's tonsils with the condition that ether, not cocaine, be used as an anesthetic. Testimony showed that the minor requested a local anesthetic upon entering the operating room, and cocaine was used. The boy died as a result of the anesthetic. In finding for the defendant, the court emphasized the contractual, rather than consensual, nature of the surgery. The court reasoned that since the deceased could have entered into a binding contract for necessaries, he could also modify a contract made on his behalf, as he did by requesting a different anesthetic. Although it is not clear that consent to surgery is a contract, it is clear that the court, in upholding the judgment for the physician, placed considerable emphasis upon the maturity of the patient and his ability to understand what he was consenting to.

The *Massachusetts* Supreme Court took into consideration a somewhat unusual factor in determining whether a minor's consent is effective. In *Masden v. Harrison,* [No. 68651 Equity Mass. (1957)], the court decided that a healthy twin, age 19, could give an effective consent to an operation in which one of his kidneys would be removed and implanted in his sick twin. After hearing a psychiatrist's report, the court found that the operation was to the healthy twin's psychological benefit, even though it might not be to his physical benefit. The court ruled that the healthy twin had sufficient capacity to understand the planned procedure and to consent.

Parental consent is no longer needed in certain cases where the minor is married or is otherwise emancipated. Approximately half the states have enacted statutes making it valid for married and emancipated minors to consent to medical and surgical procedures. For example, *New Mexico* and *Arizona* statutes specifically provide for this. A *California* statute provides for the effectiveness of a married minor's consent. Statutes making the consent of minors effective for blood donations and obstetrical care under specified circumstances have also been enacted by the *California* legislature.

Other statutes specifically provide for the effectiveness of a minor parent's consent to treatment for a child. Even in the absence of such a statute, a married minor's consent to treatment would appear to be effective where emancipation through marriage is recognized or where the maturity of the individual minor is considered. It should be noted that there are no reported cases holding a married minor's consent to treatment of a child ineffective.

Many states have recognized by legislation that there are conditions—specifically pregnancy, venereal disease, and drug dependency—for which a minor is likely to seek medical assistance without the knowledge of a parent. To require parental consent for the treatment of these conditions is to increase the risk that the minor will delay or do without treatment in order to avoid explanation to the parents.

The parents of a minor may refuse, for religious or other reasons, to consent to a medical or surgical procedure recommended for a child. Proceeding with treatment despite parental objections, in the absence of an emergency or specific statute exemptions, would almost certainly provide a basis for imposing liability. The physician could be liable for nonconsensual touching; the hospital would be liable to the same extent as for any other battery.

The ultimate decision to treat children whose parents refuse consent is for the courts to make. There is no legal justification for the hospital to proceed with treatment unless a court orders it to do so. Procedural mechanisms exist in legislation for resolving the hospital's potential conflicting role in these situations, and the hospital must take the action as provided by legislation.

CONSENT OF THE MENTALLY ILL

A person who is mentally incompetent cannot legally consent to medical or surgical treatment. For a person who has been declared legally incompetent by a judicial proceeding, the consent of the patient's legal guardian must be obtained. Where no legal guardian is available, a court that handles such matters must be asked to allow the procedure.

When a physician doubts a patient's capacity to consent, even though the patient has not been adjudged legally incompetent, the consent of the nearest relative should be obtained. In the *New York* case of *Collins v. Davis,* [44 Misc. 2d 622, 254 N.Y.S. 2d 666 (1964)], a hospital administrator sought a court order to permit a surgical operation upon an irrational adult patient whose life was in jeopardy. The consent of the patient's wife had been sought, but she refused to grant authorization for the procedure for reasons that she thought justifiable, although they were medically unsound. After the court had considered the entire situation, it pointed out that the physician and the hospital were faced with a choice: to perform the operation, contrary to the wishes of the spouse, or permit the patient to die. The court distinguished this situation from those where persons had refused medical attention or had forbidden a specific procedure for religious or other reasons. The court authorized the surgery for the reason that the patient had himself sought medical attention. The court ruled that the hospital was trying to provide the necessary medical treatment in conformity with sound medical judgment and that the spouse was interfering.

Where the patient is unable to consent, the spouse is the logical person from whom to seek consent first. But if the patient is conscious and mentally capable of giving consent for treatment, the consent of the spouse without the consent of the competent patient would not protect the physician from liability in the event that a suit was instituted by the patient for a nonconsensual touching.

THE EMERGENCY SITUATION

An emergency exists when immediate action is required to save a patient's life or to prevent permanent impairment of the patient's health. If it is impossible in an emergency to obtain the consent of the patient or someone legally authorized to give consent, the required procedure may be undertaken without any liability for failure to procure consent. In other words, an emergency removes the need for consent. This rule also applies when conditions discovered during an operation must be corrected immediately and the consent of the patient or someone authorized to give consent is not obtainable. This privilege to proceed in emergencies without consent is accorded physicians because inaction at such a time may cause greater injury to the patient and would be contrary to good medical practice.

In *Zoski v. Gaines,* [271 Mich. 1, 260 N.W. 99 (1935)], a case involving the removal of a minor child's infected tonsils without parental consent, the court stated that only in very extreme cases does a surgeon have the right to operate without consent. In this case there was no need to remove the tonsils before the parents could be consulted, although their removal at some later time would have been necessary.

Proof that a procedure will protect the life or health of the patient in the face of an immediate threat can be provided by a notation on the patient's hospital record that a consultation occurred. In *Luka v. Lowrie,* [271 Mich. 122, 136 N.W. 1106 (1912)], involving a 15-year-old boy whose left foot had been run over and crushed by a train, consultation was an important factor in determining the outcome of the case. Upon arrival at the hospital, the defending physician and four house surgeons decided it was necessary to amputate the foot. The court said it was inconceivable that, had the parents been present, they would have refused consent in the face of a determination by five physicians that amputation would save the boy's life. Thus in spite of testimony at the trial that the amputation may not have been necessary, professional consultation prior to the operation supported the assertion that a genuine emergency existed and no consent was needed.

The hospital or physician should be able to establish that under the circumstances, obtaining the consent of the patient or someone legally authorized to give consent would have meant a delay which was likely to increase the hazards. If no consent is obtained after a reasonable attempt is made, the procedure may be undertaken.

REFUSAL OF A PATIENT TO CONSENT

An adult patient who is conscious and mentally competent has the right to refuse to permit any medical or surgical procedure. This refusal must be honored whether it is grounded in doubt that the contemplated procedure will be successful, concern about the probable or possible results, lack of confidence in the surgeon, religious belief, or mere whim. Every person has the legal right to refuse to permit a touching of his body; failure to respect this right will result in liability for assault and battery.

In *Erickson v. Dilgard,* [44 Misc. 2d 27, 252 N.Y.S. 2d 705 (1962)], the court held that a competent adult patient's wishes concerning his person may not be disregarded. The court was confronted with a request by the hospital to authorize a blood transfusion over the patient's objection. The court recognized that the patient's refusal might cause his death, but would not authorize the blood transfusion, holding that a competent individual has the right to make this decision even though it may seem unreasonable to medical experts.

Failure to consent to any treatment has the same legal effect as an express prohibition of a treatment or procedure, or an express prohibition of its extension. The physician would be liable for proceeding without the patient's consent. What is more, the responsibility of the hospital and its employees is clear when it permits treatment of a patient despite the express refusal of consent. The hospital owes the duty of using reasonable care to protect the patient from touching for which consent has been expressly refused.

If the patient refuses to sign a consent form for the contemplated procedures or orally communicates a refusal of consent to the hospital's nurses, the hospital will probably be held by the courts to have received notice of the patient's refusal to consent. The hospital then has to prevent the procedure from taking place. Therefore, nurses who learn that a patient has refused contemplated treatment must communicate this knowledge to their supervisor so that the hospital can act to fulfill this duty.

RELEASE FORM

When a patient refuses to consent to a procedure for any reason, religious or otherwise, a release form should be filled out to protect the hospital and its personnel from liability for failure to perform the procedure. The patient's medical record should note when treatment was refused; the completed release form provides proof of the patient's refusal to consent. If the patient should refuse to sign the release form, this, too, should be noted.

The release form, when properly signed by the patient's spouse or nearest relative, is evidence that the medical care furnished was in accordance with the patient's wishes. When the patient is incompetent or unable to consent and the spouse or nearest relative refuses consent, it is essential that the person responsible for consent sign a release form. Where the patient is conscious and mentally competent, a release form signed by the spouse or relative is not a substitute for the patient's own release form.

A conscious, mentally competent adult patient has the right to refuse medical treatment, even when the best medical opinion deems it essential to save the patient's life. In the *Illinois* case *In re Brook's Estate,* [32 Ill. 2d 3!61, 205 N.E. 2d 435 (1965)], the court held that a competent adult patient without minor children cannot be compelled to accept a blood transfusion which she has steadfastly refused because of her religious beliefs. In this case the patient had made known her beliefs to her physician and the hospital before consenting to any medical treatment. She was aware at all times of the meaning of her decision and had signed a statement, releasing the hospital and her attending physician from liability for any consequences of her refusal to accept a blood transfusion.

Only a compelling state interest will justify interference with an individual's free exercise of religious beliefs. The Court of Appeals of the *District of Columbia* noted in *In re Osborne,* [294 A. 2d 372 (D.C. Ct. App. 1972)], that a possible overriding interest is the state's concern for the welfare of the children of patients who refuse for religious reasons to consent to treatment. However, the court found that this particular patient had made sufficient financial provision for the future well-being of his two young children, so that they would not become wards of the state if he should die. Under the circumstances, the court held that there was no compelling state interest to justify overriding the patient's intelligent and knowing refusal to consent to a transfusion because of his religious beliefs.

In some cases, the courts *have* ordered medical or surgical treatment for patients who have refused consent. *Application of the President and Directors of Georgetown College, Inc.,* [331 F. 2d 1000 (D.C. Cir., 1964)], involved a pregnant patient at the Georgetown Hospital. The hospital sought a court order authorizing blood transfusions because the patient's physicians said they were necessary to save her life. The patient and her husband had refused authorization because of their religious beliefs.

To learn whether the woman was in a mental condition to make a decision, the judge asked her what would be the effect, in terms of her religious beliefs, if the blood transfusions were authorized. Her response was that the transfusions would no longer be her responsibility. In its decision the court stressed that the woman had come to the hospital seeking medical attention and that it was convinced she wanted to live. Furthermore, according to the woman's statement, if the court undertook to authorize the transfusions without her consent, she would not be acting contrary to her religious beliefs.

The *New Jersey* Supreme Court took the position in *John F. Kennedy Memorial Hospital v. Heston,* [58 N.J. 576, 279 A. 2d 670 (1971)], that the state's power to authorize a blood transfusion does not rest upon the fact of the patient's condition or competence; it rests upon the fact of the state's compelling interest in protecting the life of its citizens, which is sufficient to justify overriding the patient's determination to refuse vital aid. The opinion also highlighted the very difficult position in which the hospital and its staff are placed when treatment is refused.

In light of these decisions, hospitals, physicians, and nurses should seek legal advice and a court ruling when refusal of treatment poses a serious threat to the patient's health. A release form signed by the patient or the spouse or nearest relative should be completed or the medical record should show any refusals to sign release forms.

Section 5
THE NURSE'S CONSENT

The nurse has two main duties with respect to a patient's consent to treatment. First, it is generally the nurse who has to fill in the consent form, take it to the patient, explain it in language that the patient can understand, and then get the patient's consent.

It is sometimes difficult to make the explanation clear, in order to satisfy the legal requirement that the patient understand, and at the same time avoid frightening the patient. At least as much discretion and care are needed for this as for any other nursing act in order to avoid overemphasis or underemphasis of risks. Thus it is preferable that the patient's consent be procured by the operating physician.

The patient may withdraw consent at any time, and the withdrawal may be oral even though the original consent was written. Therefore, after the initial consent has been obtained, the nurse must continue to be alert to the patient's condition and must relay to the hospital administration any change in the patient's consent. At the same time the nurse must distinguish between nervousness and an actual retraction of consent. In any event, the nurse should be alert to the possibility that a nonconsenting patient might be touched and a procedure completed which would later lead to an assertion of liability.

The emergency room provides the nurse with additional problems of patient consent. Because most patients who are treated in a hospital emergency room need immediate care, it is unwise for a nurse on duty in an emergency room to withhold or delay treatment while a consent form is procured, filled out, and signed. The emergency room illustrates the situation in which presence and voluntary submission to treatment constitute consent. At no time should care be delayed for paperwork, whether patient information or consent form. In these situations, consent is implied, and the nurse should see to it that immediate help is provided.

Section 6

CONSENT IMPLIED BY STATUTE

A battery is committed if a sample of a person's blood, urine, other bodily substances, or breath is taken without consent, even though the person is brought to the hospital by the police on suspicion of drunken driving. Both the nurse who withdraws the sample and the hospital may be liable for an unauthorized touching.

In some states the motor vehicle laws provide that accepting the privilege of driving upon the highways implies a person's consent to furnishing a sample of blood or urine for chemical analysis when charged with driving while intoxicated. Generally, these statutes imply authorization of a test, and an action of assault and battery will not be upheld. It is not clear, however, whether an action for battery would apply if the test were conducted after the motor vehicle operator voiced objections. The *Kansas* statute, for example, assumes consent if a person accepts the privilege of driving. But it specifically acknowledges that such consent may be withdrawn and that the person may refuse to submit to the test. Several other states acknowledge that a person may withdraw consent and have dealt with the issue of the implication when the person is unconscious at the time a sample of blood, urine, or breath is taken. One state has specifically provided that an unconscious person is considered not to have withdrawn consent to any such test. Another has provided that, at least for purposes of a criminal or civil case, it would be conclusively presumed that the person has refused to consent to and has objected to such taking. In states that have not specifically dealt with the issue of the unconscious person, the situation is not clear.

There are no reported decisions regarding the extent of hospital or personnel liability for obtaining a testing sample from a person who has not given consent when the sample has been requested by a law enforcement officer. Some states have enacted statutes which imply that court action may be brought against the individual obtaining such a sample as well as against the hospital employer. However, some statutes protect physicians, hospitals, and their employees from any liability for obtaining a blood sample from a nonconsenting individual when a police officer has requested the sample. Such a statute has been enacted in *New York*. It provides:

> §1194 *CHEMICAL TESTS* [N.Y. Vehicle and Traffic Law]
> b. No physician, registered professional nurse . . . or hospital employing such physician, registered professional nurse, . . . and no other employer of such physician, registered professional nurse . . . shall be sued or held liable for any act done or omitted in the course of withdrawing blood at the request of a police officer pursuant to this section.

In the absence of statutory protection, a procedure performed despite an individual's refusal to consent would constitute a battery. However, recovery would probably be limited to nominal damages unless physical harm resulted from negligent performance.

Most cases concerning blood, alcohol, urine, or breath tests have dealt with the issue of whether the test results were admissible as evidence in a prosecution against a defendant from whom a specimen was taken. In these cases several constitutional questions stem from the lack of the defendant's consent. In *Schmerber v. California*, [384 U.S. 757 (1966)], the defendant was placed under arrest at the hospital and blood was withdrawn by a physician for the test. The defendant had not consented to the procedure and, in fact, had objected on advice of a lawyer. In a close decision the United States Supreme Court held that when blood is withdrawn by a physician in a medically acceptable manner, the procedure does not offend the court's "sense of justice," nor does it deny the defendant the legal rights guaranteed by the Fourteenth Amendment. The majority of judges agreed that evidence derived from a blood test, although incriminating and obtained under duress, did not constitute testimony or some communicative act or writing. Thus the results of such a test were admissible, and admitting them did not violate the defendant's right against self-incrimination.

The Court also considered the results of a blood test in terms of the Fourth Amendment, which prohibits unreasonable search and seizure. The evidence of the defendant's condition prior to the blood-sampling procedure was viewed by the Court as sufficient to establish probable cause for the police officer to arrest the defendant on a charge of driving while intoxicated. Once a valid arrest has been made, search of a suspect is permitted if the search is reasonable. The Court held that the procedure used to withdraw the blood was performed according to accepted medical standards by a competent person and therefore met the test of reasonableness.

However, if the purpose for the withdrawal of blood is misrepresented, consent for the procedure may not be effective, thereby making the results of the test inadmissible and laying the basis for imposing tort liability.

It must also be recognized that, even though the admission of test results as evidence against a defendant in a criminal proceeding may not violate constitutional rights, the hospital employee who withdraws the blood might still be liable for an unauthorized touching.

MEDICAL RECORDS

Proper recording of the facts of a patient's illness, symptoms, diagnosis, and treatment is one of the most important functions in furnishing modern medical and hospital care. Nurses and physicians are primarily charged with the responsibility of keeping accurate and up-to-date medical records. All hospital personnel who have access to medical records have both a legal and an ethical obligation to protect the confidentiality of the information in the records. For these and other reasons, it is important that the nurse know what the medical records are and what significance they have in the law.

Section 1
IMPORTANCE

Medical records are maintained primarily to provide accurate and complete information about the care and treatment of patients. They are also the principal means of communication between physician and nurse in matters relating to patient care, and they serve as a basis for planning the course of treatment. The records show the extent and quality of care, both for statistical purposes and for research and education, and they may be used for later review, study, and evaluation of the care rendered the patient. In addition, the records provide information for billing and reports. Finally, the records are a valuable aid in court proceedings.

The nurse's handling of medical records is particularly important because the nurse is the one medical professional the patient sees more than any other. Consequently, the nurse is in a position to keep constant watch over the patient's illness, response to medication, display of pain and discomfort, and general condition. The patient's care as well as the nurse's observations should be recorded fully, factually, and promptly. No nurse should attempt to make a diagnosis, even if the conclusions seem obvious.

Also, the nurse should promptly and accurately comply with the orders the physician writes in the record and should check, in case of doubt, to make certain that the order is correct and that it has not already been completed.

Section 2

CONTENTS

The medical record is a complete, accurate, up-to-date report of the medical history, condition, and treatment of each patient and the result of the hospitalization.

The medical record is composed of at least two distinct parts, each of which may be made up of several types of itemizations and forms. The first part is compiled in the ordinary case upon admission; it details the pertinent particulars of the patient's history such as name, age, and reason for admission. The second part is the clinical record, which is a continuing history of the treatment given to the patient while in the hospital. The information in this part is prescribed by state licensing rules and regulations. Usually, it must contain the patient's physical history, complaint, temperature chart, admitting diagnosis, later diagnoses, consultations, medical notes, laboratory reports of tests, X-ray readings, surgical or delivery records (including anesthesia reports, operative procedures, and findings), nurses' notes, summaries, condition of the patient at time of discharge, autopsy findings, and so forth. This record is maintained continually by the doctors and nurses who attend the patient. In most states both doctors and nurses must sign or initial the record.

Legislation and regulations concerning medical records vary from state to state. Some states detail the information to be recorded, other states specify the broad areas of information required concerning the patient's treatment, and some states simply declare that the medical record shall be adequate, accurate, or complete. State hospital licensure rules and regulations may also set out requirements and standards for the maintenance, handling, signing, filing, and retention of medical records.

In addition to specific requirements, all licensing regulations say that all records must be accurate and complete. What is more, the Joint Commission on Accreditation of Hospitals and several licensing regulations require prompt completion of records after the discharge of patients. Persistent failure to conform to a medical staff rule requiring the physician to complete records promptly was held in *Board of Trustees of Memorial Hospital v. Pratt,* [72 Wyo. 120, 262 P. 2d 682 (1953)], to provide a basis for suspending a staff member. Almost all regulations require that the practitioners sign the record. Some require that all orders be signed; others merely refer to the signing of the completed record.

Section 3

THE MEDICAL RECORD IN LEGAL PROCEEDINGS

The increasing incidence of personal injury suits and the expanding acceptance of life, accident, and health insurance have made medical records important evidence in legal proceedings. These records aid police investigations, provide information for determining the cause of death, and indicate the extent of injury in workmen's compensation or personal injury proceedings.

When nurses or physicians are called as witnesses in a proceeding, they are permitted to refresh their recollections of the facts and circumstances of a particular case by referring to the record. Courts recognize that it is impossible for a medical witness to remember the details of every patient's treatment, and the record may therefore be used as an aid in relating the facts. In this situation the record stimulates the recall of the witness who testifies under oath and is subject to cross-examination.

The medical record itself may be admitted into evidence in legal proceedings. In this situation, the record is not under oath and is not subject to cross-examination. In order for medical record information to be allowed in evidence, the court must be assurred that the information is accurate, that it was recorded at the time the event took place, and that it was not recorded in anticipation of the particular legal proceeding. In short, while it is recognized that witnesses may refresh their memories and that records may be admitted into evidence, there is nevertheless a need for assurance that the information is trustworthy.

When a medical record is introduced, its custodian, usually the medical record librarian, must testify to the manner in which the record was made and the way in which it is protected from unauthorized handling and change. It is to be noted that whether such records and other documents are admitted or excluded is governed by the rules of evidence. Thus whether the records are admissible depends on the facts and circumstances of the particular case.

Whatever the situation, it is clear that the record must be complete, accurate, and timely. If it can be shown that the record is inaccurate or incomplete or that it was made long after the event it purports to record, it will not be accepted.

Section 4

CONFIDENTIAL COMMUNICATIONS

Under certain circumstances, the medical record may not be admitted into evidence in a court proceeding because the court deems it to be a confidential communication between the patient and the physician and therefore protected from disclosure.

One party to a relationship based on trust and confidence may give information to the other party in a situation and under circumstances which legally imply that the information should remain undisclosed. The information given is called a confidential communication. In our legal system, the relationship between physician and patient is accorded the protection of confidential communications. Sometimes the privilege of confidential communications also extends to the nurse.

Medical information may be gained by examination, treatment, observation, or conversation. The nurse, as well as the physician, has a clear moral obligation to keep secret any information relating to a patient's illness or treatment which is learned during the course of professional duties, unless the nurse is authorized by the patient to disclose the information or is ordered by a court to do so.

The confidentiality of communications in a medical situation is a principal tenet of the nursing code of professional ethics. There are also state statutes that forbid physicians, dentists, and other health practitioners from disclosing, without the patient's consent, any information acquired during the course of caring for a patient. Some of the statutes expressly include disclosures made to a professional, registered, or trained nurse, which means the nurse cannot be forced to testify in a legal proceeding about information obtained while caring for the patient. However, in most pertinent state statutes, nurses are not subject to the restrictions concerning revelation of confidential communications. The courts of a few states have held that, by implication, these statutes include nurses who are assisting or acting under the direction of a physician who treats the patient.

Although the statutory protection of information obtained in the physician-patient relationship applies only to courtroom testimony, there is a general belief that some protection should be afforded the personal and private revelations of the patient to the physician so that the revelations will not be subject to general dissemination in the community. The physician has an ethical duty not to disclsoe information received from the patient. Most states limit the protection to information furnished the physician that is necessary to enable treatment of the patient, and legislation often limits the physician-patient privilege to certain kinds of legal actions. The privilege may be applied to information in hospital records as well as to communications to physicians. To a lesser extent, these principles also apply to nurses working directly under physicians.

In the operation of a hospital and the provision of patient care, staff physicians and hospital personnel may have to use information from the records. Moreover, physicians, residents, interns, nurses, and other personnel may consult the records for the purposes of research, statistical evaluation, and education. However, if the information so obtained is not kept confidential, the hospital may be held liable.

If the information from medical records is disclosed, without a court order or statutory authority to do so and without the patient's consent, the hospital or its employees may be held liable for damages if the patient's interests are harmed. Patients have alleged injury in these situations on the grounds of defamation or invasion of their right to privacy.

The restriction on disclosing information obtained in a confidential relationship ordinarily does not apply to criminal matters, such as attempted suicide or the unlawful dispensing or taking of narcotic drugs. Likewise, the patient may waive the privilege by actions or words. For example, a patient who testifies about an illness can no longer claim protection for the information.

Section 5

NEGLIGENCE

The medical record must be both accurate and complete. Failure to comply with the minimum record maintenance standards set out in state statutes may cause the revocation of medical personnel licenses or hospital accreditation.

In addition, liability may be found against a hospital for the breach of a duty to maintain accurate records. In *Hansch v. Hackett,* [190 Wash. 97, 66 P. 2d 1129 (1937)], the *Washington* Supreme Court imposed liability on a hospital for an attending nurse's failure to observe and record the symptoms of eclampsia. The court attributed the patient's subsequent death to this failure because the physician might have ordered the prompt and necessary treatment if the information had been available. In a *Louisiana* case, *Favalora v. Aetna Casualty & Surety Co.,* [144 So. 2d 544 (La. Ct. App. 1962)], the hospital and radiologist were held liable for injuries sustained by an elderly patient who fainted and fell while being X-rayed. The hospital was liable under *respondeat superior* for the failure of a nurse to complete the medical history portion of the X-ray requisition. The basis of the radiologist's liability was the failure to acquaint himself with the patient's history before he commenced the examination.

A nurse is also responsible for making the proper inquiry if there is uncertainty about the accuracy of an order in the record. In the *Louisiana* case of *Norton v. Argonaut Insurance Co.,* [111 So. 2d 249 (La. Ct. App. 1962)], the court focused attention upon the responsibility of a nurse to obtain clarification of an apparently erroneous order from the patient's physician. The medication order of the attending physician as entered in the chart was incomplete and subject to misinterpretation. Believing the order to be incorrect because of the dosage, the nurse asked two physicians present in the ward whether the medication should be given as ordered. The two physicians did not interpret the order as the nurse did and therefore did not share the same concern. They told the nurse that the attending physician's instructions did not appear out of line. The nurse did not contact the attending physician but instead administered the misinterpreted dosage of medication. As a result the patient died from a fatal overdose of the medication. The court upheld the jury's finding that the nurse had been negligent in failing to get in touch with the attending physician before giving the medication. The nurse was held liable, as was the physician who wrote the ambiguous order that led to the fatal dose.

In discussing the standard of care expected of a nurse who encounters an apparently erroneous order, the court stated:

> Not only was [the nurse] unfamiliar with the medicine in question, but she also violated what has been shown to be the rule generally practiced by the members of the nursing profession in the community and which rule, we might add, strikes us as being most reasonable and prudent, namely, the practice of calling the prescribing physician when in doubt about an order for medication. True, [she] attempted to verify the order by inquiring of [two physicians] but evidently there was a complete lack of communication with these individuals. The record leaves no doubt but that neither [physician] was made aware of just what [the nurse] intended to administer.

The court noted further:

> For obvious reasons we believe it the duty of a nurse when in doubt about an order for medication to make absolutely certain what the doctor intended both as to dosage and route. In the case at bar the evidence leaves not the slightest doubt that whereas nurses in the locality do at times consult any available physician, it appears equally certain that all of the nurses who testified herein agree that the better practice (and the one which they follow) is to consult the prescribing physician when in doubt about an order for medication.

Thus clarification was not sought from the physician who wrote the order, and this departure from the standard of competent nursing practice provided the basis for holding the nurse liable for negligence.

DRUGS AND MEDICATIONS

A NURSE IS REQUIRED TO HANDLE AND ADMINISTER MANY DRUGS THAT ARE DIS-
pensed by a hospital pharmacy or prescribed by a physician. The medications may range from simple aspirin to the latest experimental drugs.
Every nurse has a legal duty to handle these drugs in the manner prescribed by statute.

Section 1
PHARMACY ACTS

All states have promulgated statutes specifying that pharmacy may be
practiced only by persons who are legally licensed. The individual statutes
also define those activities that constitute the practice of pharmacy.
Although the definitions vary from state to state, certain activities are
included in each state's definition.

Essentially, the practice of pharmacy includes preparing, compounding,
dispensing, and retailing drugs, medicines, prescriptions, chemicals, and
poisons. These activities may be carried out only by a pharamacist with a
state license or by a person exempted from the provisions of the state's
pharmacy statute. A physician is such an exempted person when he compounds, dispenses, or administers medicines or drugs to patients during his
practice. The nurse is also exempt from the prohibitions of the various
pharmacy statutes when administering a medicine or a drug to a patient
upon an oral or written order of a physician. Any nurse who administered
a drug without an order from a physician would be in violation of the
state's pharmacy statute. A nurse is not exempted from the pharmacy act
when acting without proper authorization.

To adhere to the tenets of the state pharmacy acts, a nurse should
understand what specific activities constitute the compounding, dispensing, and retailing of pharmaceutical items. *Compounding* is the

combining and mixing of drugs, chemicals, or poisons. For example, a pharmacist compounds a drug by filling a physician's prescription; this entails preparing and mixing the prescribed articles.

Dispensing is defined as delivering, distributing, disposing, or giving away a drug, medicine, prescription, chemical, or poison. Although some state statutes authorize a nurse to dispense drugs in certain instances, most states do not provide specific statutory authorization for this. Theoretically, a nurse may not dispense drugs in states that do not provide specific authorization. However, in many hospitals it is the general practice and custom to allow nurses to enter the hospital pharmacy and obtain drugs or remove drugs from the hospital's floor stock cabinet in order to carry out a physician's orders. Despite this generally accepted practice, there has been little modification by state legislatures of the restrictions in the state pharmacy acts.

Retailing is simply the act of selling or trading a drug, medicine, prescription, chemical, or poison.

The articles that are compounded and dispensed by a pharmacist are drugs, medicines, prescriptions, chemicals, and poisons. The definition of *drug* in most state statutes is similar to the one found in the Federal Food, Drug, and Cosmetic Act; this law says that drugs are articles recognized in the official United States Pharmacopoeia, official Homeopathic Pharmacopoeia of the United States, or official National Formulary, or their supplements, and articles (other than food) intended to affect the structure or function of the body of man or other animals.

Applying this definition, courts have decided that aspirin, laxatives, vitamin and mineral capsules, honey, and whole human blood can be drugs under certain circumstances. Therefore, when handling these drugs the nurse should be aware that they cannot be dispensed, compounded, or retailed.

Section 2

CONTROLLED SUBSTANCES

FEDERAL REGULATION

The Comprehensive Drug Abuse Prevention and Control Act of 1970, commonly known as the Controlled Substances Act, was signed into law on October 27, 1970. Virtually all earlier federal laws dealing with narcotics, depressants, stimulants, and hallucinogens were replaced by this law. The Act also deals with hospital distribution systems, rehabilitation projects under community mental health programs, research in and medical treatment of drug abuse and addiction, and importation and exportation of controlled substances.

A number of definitions and concepts affecting the operative provisions of the law are especially important to nurses. Only practitioners are permitted to dispense or conduct research with controlled substances. Practitioners are defined in these words:

§ 802

* * * *

(20) The term "practitioner" means a physician, dentist, veterinarian, scientific investigator, pharmacy, hospital, or other person licensed, registered, or otherwise permitted, by the United States or the jurisdiction in which he practices or does research, to distribute, dispense . . . administer . . . a controlled substance in the course of professional practice or research.

* * * *

Thus, once properly licensed or registered, practitioners are authorized to dispense controlled substances. The term "dispense" is defined as follows:

§802

* * * *

(10) The term "dispense" means to deliver a controlled substance to an ultimate user or research subject by, or pursuant to the lawful order of, a practitioner, including the prescribing and administering of a controlled substance. . . .

* * * *

Therefore, one registered to dispense may prescribe, administer, or dispense (in the traditional sense) under the Controlled Substances Act, if permitted to do so under state law. The term "administer" is defined thus:

§802

* * * *

(2) The term "administer" refers to the direct application of a controlled substance to the body of a patient or research subject by—

(A) a practitioner (or in his presence, by his authorized agent), or

(B) the patient or research subject at the direction and in the presence of the practitioner, whether such application be by injection, inhalation, ingestion, or any other means.

* * * *

These sections of the Controlled Substance Act indicate that a nurse is prohibited from dispensing or prescribing controlled substances. However, a nurse is authorized to administer a controlled substance at the direction and in the presence of a practitioner. Thus a nurse may follow a physician's oral and written orders to administer a quantity of a drug at a specified time to the proper patient.

Practitioners must register with the government in accordance with the provisions of the Act. Each registrant must take a physical inventory every two years and maintain inventory records, but a perpetual inventory is not required. However, a separate inventory is compulsory for each registered location and for each registered independent activity. In addition to inventory records, each registrant must maintain complete and accurate records of all controlled substances received and disposed of.

All registrants must provide effective controls and procedures to guard against theft and diversion of controlled substances. For example, a hospital's central storage should be under the direct control and supervision of the pharmacist. Only authorized personnel should have access to the area. When controlled substances are stored at nursing units, they too should be kept securely locked, and only authorized personnel should have access to these drugs.

The controlled substances listed in Schedules I through IV of the Act include narcotics, depressants, stimulants, and hallucinogens.

STATE REGULATION

Until the enactment of the Controlled Substances Act, most states had adopted some version of the Uniform Narcotic Drug Act. Since Congress amended the federal law, the states have been steadily replacing their narcotic and depressant-stimulant laws with "mini" controlled substances acts. Thus far, more than two-thirds of the states have enacted such legislation.

The new state laws are based upon the Uniform Controlled Substances Act, which in turn is based upon the federal Controlled Substances Act. However, a number of states have modified the uniform act in various ways, and the law of each state must be examined before legal conclusions can be reached. The variations include prescription requirements and penalties for violations.

Section 3

DRUGS

FEDERAL REGULATION

Almost all the drugs handled and administered by a nurse are rigidly regulated, and it is therefore imperative that every nurse who is authorized to deal with these drugs understand the manner in which they are regulated.

Drugs, Devices, and Cosmetics. The Food, Drug, and Cosmetic Act applies to the purity, labeling, potency, safety, and effectiveness of various products in varying degree depending on how they are classified; therefore, it is important to distinguish them. The Federal Food, Drug, and Cosmetic Act and federal regulations promulgated under the Act should be consulted. There has been considerable litigation in this area, and these decisions must be taken into account.

A number of items used by medical personnel that have been held to be drugs, although they may not seem to be drugs to a casual observer, include antibiotic sensitivity discs used in laboratory procedures to determine the inhibiting ability of various antibiotics on sample microorganisms, diagnostic preparations listed in official compendia, and certain sutures used for tying off blood vessels during surgical procedures. Whole human blood has also been held to be a drug within the meaning of the Food, Drug, and Cosmetic Act and so have plastic bags used for the storage of blood and other intravenous substances.

The Food and Drug Administration now has a special office to deal specifically with devices on the market, and special attention will be given to products affecting life itself, such as pacemakers. Legislative proposals are being considered in this problem area.

New and Investigational Drugs. Critical in analyzing the effect of the operative provision of the Food, Drug, and Cosmetic Act is the definition of "new drug." The law and regulations establish an elaborate procedure for determining whether a new drug is safe and effective. As part of this procedure, the Food and Drug Administration may condition its approval to market a new drug upon specified stipulations.

Some of the conditions that have caused concern are indications for use or dosage levels which may be listed in the official labeling. Specifically, a problem may arise if a physician prescribes a new drug for a condition or in a dosage other than those in the approved labeling, and a pharmacist is asked to dispense the drug and a nurse to administer it. As a general rule, physicians may prescribe and pharmacists may dispense new drugs for uses, in dosages, or in regimens different from those set forth in a drug's approved labeling without violation of the law.

The general law of negligence is the law that governs in cases involving the use of new drugs in a way other than the ones provided for in the official labeling. For example, in applying these principles to hospital practice, it appears prudent for a pharmacist to question a physician who prescribes a drug in a manner that deviates substantially from the package insert. In really questionable cases, an acknowledgment and assumption of liability form could be obtained from the physician to protect the pharmacist and hospital in the event of any subsequent liability suit.

Labeling and Manufacturing. Labeling specifications are set forth in the Food, Drug, and Cosmetic Act and in regulations pursuant to the Act.

These labeling and prescription requirements are of major importance to the practice of hospital pharmacy.

When prescription drugs are ordered in writing there is no particular problem. The physician either fills out a prescription or writes an order on the patient's chart, which serves as the written prescription. However, if an oral order is given for the drug, the Act states that such prescriptions must be ". . . reduced promptly to writing and filed by the pharmacist. . . ." Refills for such drugs. must be treated likewise. Thus the validity of hospital practice concerning drug orders telephoned to personnel other than pharmacists is questionable under the Act.

Every person who owns or operates any establishment engaged in the interstate or intrastate manufacture, preparation, propagation, compounding, or processing of drugs must register his name, place of business, and all such establishments with the Secretary of Health, Education and Welfare. The words "manufacture, preparation, propagation, compounding, or processing" include repackaging or otherwise changing the container, wrapper, or labeling of drugs for distribution to others who will make final sale or distribution to the ultimate consumer.

In addition to these registration requirements there are other manufacturing obligations under the Act, such as maintaining certain records, filing specified reports, and tolerating periodic plant inspections.

In 1972, Congress amended the Food, Drug, and Cosmetic Act to require all manufacturers to file with the government a list of all drugs they manufacture. The issue of importance to the current practice of pharmacy arising under this amendment is whether the compounding of drugs and pharmaceuticals in large quantities or the unit dose packaging and relabeling of drugs constitutes manufacturing under the Act. For example, a hospital pharmacy that prepares large quantities of drugs for use by the institution's patients would appear to be exempt. On the other hand, if the hospital pharmacy were supplying these compounded or repackaged drugs to other institutions or pharmacies under circumstances other than emergencies, it would not be exempt.

STATE REGULATION

Although certain provisions of the Federal Food, Drug, and Cosmetic Act specifically apply to intrastate commerce insofar as drugs are concerned, Congress has at various times specifically provided for the applicability of state law. Accordingly, most states now have food, drug, and cosmetic laws based primarily upon the Uniform State Food, Drug, and Cosmetic Bill. State laws vary in specific details and must be consulted in making a determination as to whether a specific course of conduct is in compliance with all applicable laws.

Section 4
LIABILITY

Violation of the pharmacy acts may be evidence of negligence, but there has been no court decision holding a nurse negligent because the action which resulted in harm was also in violation of the state pharmacy act.

Although state pharmacy acts define the minimum qualifications for dispensing drugs, nurse licensing laws may also provide standards of practice relevant to drug dispensing. In *Barber v. Reinking,* [68 Wash. 2d 122, 411 P. 2d 861 (1966)], the court found that a practical nurse's violation of the state Nurse Practice Act, which provided that only a licensed professional nurse could administer an inoculation, was relevant evidence of negligence. The nurse, concerned over the large number of patients waiting in the physician's office, administered a polio booster shot to a two-year-old child. The needle broke in the child's buttock and was not removed until nine months later. The practical nurse was found negligent by the court.

Violation of a licensing statute can produce liability only when it can be proved that the violation was the cause of the harm. If it is foreseeable that harm may result if an unlicensed person performs acts that are restricted to licensed persons with professional training and experience, and if an unlicensed person performs such an act and in fact causes harm, liability will follow. However, when no harm follows the violation of a licensing statute, the legal issue requires that the appropriate state licensing board decide whether to prosecute for violation of the statute.

INTENTIONAL WRONGS

ALTHOUGH MOST INCIDENTS RAISING ISSUES OF A NURSE'S LIABILITY CONCERN HARM allegedly resulting from negligence, a nurse may also be liable for intentional wrongs. Intentional tortious conduct (in other words, conduct implying a civil wrong) that may arise in the context of patient care includes assault, battery, false imprisonment, invasion of privacy, libel, and slander.

There are two major differences between intentional and negligent wrongs. One is the factor of intent, which is present in intentional but not in negligent wrongs. The second difference is less obvious. An intentional wrong always involves a willful act which violates another's rights; a negligent wrong may not involve an act at all. In a situation involving negligence, a person may be held liable for not acting in the way that a reasonably prudent person would have acted. Thus negligence can be a failure to act as well as a careless act.

Section I

BATTERY

A battery is an intentional, unconsented touching of another's person. The principle upon which liability is based is an individual's right to be free from invasion of his person. What is important, when a battery occurs, is that a right has been invaded; and the law provides a remedy to the individual for the interference. Therefore, the injured person can sue a wrongdoer for the damages suffered. Even where benefits are incurred or no actual harm results, the law presumes a compensable injury to the person by the fact that the battery occurred.

In the health context, the principle of law having to do with battery and the requirement of consent to medical and surgical procedures are of critical importance. Liability of hospitals, physicians, and nurses for acts of battery is most common in situations involving patient consent to medical and surgical procedures. It is inevitable that a patient in a hospital will be touched by many persons for many reasons. Procedures ranging from surgery to taking X-rays involve some touching of a patient. Even the administration of some medications may entail touching. Therefore, medical and surgical procedures must be authorized by the patient. If they are not authorized, the person performing the procedure will be subject to an action for battery.

It is of no legal importance that a procedure constituting a battery has improved the patient's health. If there was no patient consent to the touching, the patient may be entitled to damages.

Section 2

FALSE IMPRISONMENT

False imprisonment is the unlawful restraint of an individual's personal liberty or the unlawful detention of an individual. Actual physical force is not necessary to constitute a false imprisonment. All that is necessary is a reasonable fear that force, which may be implied by words, threats, or gestures, will be used to detain the individual.

Not allowing a patient to leave a hospital until all bills have been paid, may constitute false imprisonment. However, hospitals or nurses are not liable for false imprisonment if they compel a patient with a contagious disease to stay in the hospital. Mentally ill patients may also be kept in the hospital if there is a danger that they will take their own lives or jeopardize the lives and property of others. But mental illness alone is not sufficient reason to detain a patient. Those who are mentally ill or insane can be restrained only if they present a danger to themselves to others, or to property.

How much force can be used to restrain a patient? Only as much as is reasonable under the circumstances. Excessive force may produce liability for a battery for the hospital and the nurse. If a mentally ill patient has to remain in the hospital, procedures should begin immediately to provide commitment to a mental institution.

A patient of sound mind who needs further medical attention but wants to go home should not be detained merely because the medical staff believes the patient would benefit from further hospitalization. The nature of the patient's condition and its probable consequences should be explained. The insistence on leaving should be noted on the medical record, and the patient should be asked to sign a form releasing the hospital from liability for harm resulting from premature departure. In this situation, it is important to note that the patient does not actually have to be constrained to be falsely imprisoned. A threat of restraint which the patient may reasonably expect to be carried out might be enough to constitute false imprisonment.

Section 3
INVASION OF PRIVACY

The right of privacy, as recognized by the law, is the right to be left alone—the right to be free from unwarranted publicity and exposure to public view as well as the right to live one's life without having one's name, picture, or private affairs made public against one's will. Hospitals, physicians, and nurses may become liable for invasion of privacy if they divulge information from a patient's medical record to improper sources or if they commit unwarranted intrusions into the patient's personal affairs.

Hospitals could be held liable under this principle if they were responsible for the unwarranted intrusion into the private affairs of a patient. For example, a hospital was sued for allowing pictures to be taken of a malformed dead child. In another case, a doctor who took pictures of a patient's disfigured face while she was in extreme pain and semiconscious was legally restrained from developing or making prints of the negatives.

The information on a patient's chart is confidential and cannot be disclosed without the patient's permission. Nurses, who come into possession of the most intimate and personal information about patients, have both a legal and an ethical duty not to reveal confidential communications. The legal duty arises because the law recognizes a right to privacy, and to protect this right there is a corresponding duty to obey. The ethical duty is broader and applies at all times.

There *are* occasions when a nurse has a legal obligation or duty to disclose information. The reporting of communicable diseases, gunshot wounds, child abuse, and other matters is required by law.

There are also certain exceptions to the right of privacy. Virtually all the doings of a person who is a public figure are of legitimate interest to the public. Relatively obscure people may voluntarily take certain actions to bring themselves before the public or may be involved in newsworthy occurrences. A patient may also waive the right to privacy by actions or words.

The liberty extended to the publication of personal matters, names, or photographs varies. Public figures probably will not be heard to complain if their lives are given publicity; and ordinary citizens who voluntarily adopt a course of conduct which is newsworthy have no grounds for complaint if the activity is reported along with their names and pictures. Generally, the subject of a newsworthy occurrence cannot complain if the occurrence is reported in a newspaper along with his picture, but the identity of the subject loses importance as time passes and cannot be exploited by unwarranted publication.

Nurses should not allow pictures to be taken without the patient's consent. Furthermore, every hospital should implement rules and policies outlining the freedom permitted visitors in the hospital. If any visitor should try to roam around, peeking into rooms or reading charts, nurses should prevent these invasions lest the hospital be held liable.

Section 4

DEFAMATION

Defamation is defined as written or oral communication, to someone other than the person defamed, matters concerning a living person which tend to injure that person's reputation. By tradition, libel is the written form and slander the oral form of defamation. To be an actionable wrong, defamation must be communicated to a third person. Defamatory statements communicated only to the injured party are not grounds for an action.

No proof of actual damage is needed in order for libel to be actionable. With slander, on the other hand, actual damage must be proved by the person bringing suit. There are four generally recognized exceptions when no proof of any actual harm to reputation is required in order to recover damages: accusing someone of a crime; accusing someone of having a loathsome disease; using words which affect a person's profession or business; and calling a woman unchaste.

The *Georgia* case of *Barry v. Baugh,* [111 Ga. App. 813, 143 S.E. 2d 489 (1965)], considered one of these exceptions: slandering a person professionally. In this case a nurse brought a defamation action, charging that a physician had slandered her in the course of a consultation concerning the commitment of her husband to a mental institution. During a telephone conversation with a county official, the physician referred to the nurse as "crazy." As a result of this statement, the nurse requested damages for mental pain, shock, fright, humiliation, and embarrassment. The nurse alleged that, if the physician's statements were made known to the public, her job and reputation would be adversely affected. The court held that the physician's statement concerning the nurse did not constitute slander because the physician was not referring to the nurse in a professional capacity.

When any allegedly defamatory words refer to a person in a professional capacity, the professional need not show that the words caused damage. It is presumed that any slanderous reference to someone's professional capacity is damaging, and the plaintiff therefore, has no need to prove damage. In this case, however, since the court held that the physician's statement did not refer to the nurse in her professional capacity, the plaintiff had to demonstrate damage in order to recover. The plaintiff was unable to show damage of this kind and therefore lost the case.

A nurse is legally protected against libel when complying with a law requiring a report of venereal or other diseases which might be considered "loathsome."

Essentially, there are two defenses to a defamation action: truth and privilege. When a person has said something that is damaging to another person's reputation, the person making the statement will not be liable for defamation if it can be shown that the statement was true. A privileged communication is one which might be defamatory under different circumstances, but is not because of a higher duty with which the person making the communication is charged. The person making the communication must also do so in good faith, on the proper occasion, in the proper manner, and to a person who has a legitimate reason to receive the information.

The defense of privilege is illustrated in the case of *Judge v. Rockford Memorial Hospital,* [17 Ill. App. 2d 365, 150 N.E. 2d 202 (1958)]. A nurse brought an action for libel based on a letter written to a nurse's professional registry by the director of nurses at the hospital where the nurse had done private duty work. In the letter the director of nurses stated that the hospital did not wish to have the nurse's services available to them as a result of certain losses of narcotics during times when this particular nurse was on duty. The court refused the nurse recovery. Since the director of nurses had a legal duty to make the communication in the interests of society, the director's letter constituted a privileged communication. Therefore, the court held, because the letter was privileged it did not constitute libel.

PART II

THE NURSE AND HER EMPLOYER

LICENSING LAWS AND SCOPE OF PRACTICE

A NURSE MAY DISCOVER THAT THE PROCEDURE PERMITTED BY THE LICENSING authority and those required by the employer are different. These potential conflicts deal with issues concerning a nurse's "scope of practice"—in other words, the nurse's tasks as against the tasks of other health professionals.

The consequences to a nurse for exceeding the scope of practice can be severe. The nurse may be accused of a violation of licensure provisions or of performing tasks that are statutorily reserved for a physician. However, in view of increasingly complex medical procedures and hospital organization, it has become more difficult to distinguish the tasks that are clearly reserved for the physician from those that may be performed by the professional nurse.

Section 1

NURSE LICENSING LAWS

In general terms, licensure can be defined as the process by which some competent authority grants permission to a qualified individual or entity to perform certain specified activities which would be illegal without a license. As it applies to health personnel, licensure refers to the process by which licensing boards, agencies, or departments of the several states grant, to individuals who meet certain predetermined standards, the legal right to practice a health profession and/or to use a specified health practitioner's title.

The commonly stated objectives of licensing laws are to limit and control admission into the various health occupations and to protect the public from unqualified practitioners by promulgating and enforcing standards of practice within the professions.

The authority of states to license health care practitioners is found in their police or regulating power. This permits the states to regulate such occupations as may affect the public health, morals, and welfare; however, this regulating power does not extend to occupations which do not involve the public interest. Implicit in the power to license is the authority to collect license fees, establish standards of practice, require certain qualifications of applicants, and impose on applicants such other requirements as may be necessary to protect the general welfare. This authority, which is vested in the legislature, may be delegated to political subdivisions or state boards, agencies, and departments. In some instances the scope of the delegated power is made quite specific in the legislation; in others, the licensing authority may have wide discretion in performing its functions. In either case, however, the authority granted by the legislature may not be exceeded.

LICENSING BOARD

The common organizational pattern of nurse licensing authority in each state is to establish a separate board, organized and operated within the guidelines of specific legislation, to license all professional and practical nurses. Each board is in turn responsible for the determination of eligibility for initial licensing and relicensing; for the enforcement of licensing statutes, including suspension, revocation, and restoration of licenses; and for the approval and supervision of training institutions.

The governor of the state generally appoints the members of the nurse licensing board. These selections are made from a list of names submitted by professional associations that represent nurses. Many licensing acts require this advisory input from the associations. But even where this is not a statutory requirement, most governors solicit recommendations from the associations before making their selections.

The number of members on the nurse licensing boards ranges from 3 to 20, although the great majority of boards have no more than 10 members. Usually the members have a direct interest in the areas of nursing which they regulate, and often the statutes require that board members must have practiced in the state for a minimum number of years.

Recently there has been a trend toward placing members of the general public on licensing boards so as to give some representation to nonprofessional interests; however, this trend has been slight and is generally perceived as a token gesture.

REQUIREMENTS FOR LICENSURE

Formal vocational training is necessary for nurse licensure in all states. The requirements of courses vary, but all courses must be completed at board-approved schools or institutions. Although many state nurse licensing boards still adhere to their own standards for accreditation, an increasing number of boards now accept standards established by professional nursing associations and national accrediting agencies. This trend toward application of a national standard has tended to standardize the program of instruction at nursing schools.

Many nurse licensing acts permit the substitution of actual work experience for certain educational requirements. This provision makes manifest a recognition of the value of experience as an alternative to formal education and facilitates the licensing of greater numbers of qualified personnel.

For nurse licensure each state requires that the applicant pass an examination—usually written, although it may be oral, practical, or a combination, and usually administered twice a year. The examinations may be formulated completely by the nurse licensing board or they may consist in whole or part of material prepared by professional examination services or national examining boards. Some states will waive their written examination for applicants who present a certificate from a national nursing examining board.

The nurse licensing statutes also specify certain personal qualifications: minimum age, most often 21; demonstration of good moral character; and U.S. citizenship or a filed declaration of intent to become a U.S. citizen.

SPECIAL LICENSING PROCEDURES

Because each state has its own nurse licensing statutes, boards have had to deal with the problem of licensing nurses who have qualified in other states. Generally there are four methods by which boards license out-of-state licentiates: reciprocity, endorsement, examination, or waiver.

Reciprocity may be a formal or informal agreement between states whereby a nurse licensing board in one state will recognize licensees of another state if the board of that state will extend reciprocal recognition to licensees from the first state. To have reciprocity, the initial licensing requirements of the two states must be essentially equivalent.

While some nurse licensing boards use the term "endorsement" interchangeably with "reciprocity" the two words actually have different meanings. In licensing by *endorsement,* boards determine whether the out-of-state nurse's qualifications were equivalent to their own state requirements at the time of initial licensure. Many states make it a condition for endorsement that the qualifying examination taken in the other state be comparable to their own. As with reciprocity, endorsement becomes much easier where uniform qualification standards are applied by the different states. The trend toward national nursing examinations and national standards for schools of nursing has simplified both endorsement and reciprocity licensure. As the trend continues, the mobility of nurses will increase.

Licensing out-of-state nurses by *waiver* and *examination* is much less common than by reciprocity and endorsement. Where applicants do not meet all the requirements for licensure, but have equivalent qualifications, the specific educational, experience, or examination prerequisities may be waived. Some states will not recognize out-of-state licentiates and make it mandatory that all applicants pass the regular examination as well as fulfill the other requirements for initial licensure.

A majority of the states grant temporary licenses for nurses. These licenses may be given pending a decision by the board on permanent licensure or may be issued to out-of-state nurses who intend to be in a jurisdiction for only a limited time.

For the most part, nurse licensing boards are quite cautious in licensing persons educated in foreign countries. On the whole, Canadian-trained professionals are treated the same as graduates of U.S. schools because of the quick ascertainability of educational quality there. But graduates of schools in most other foreign countries are more carefully scrutinized and are required to meet the same qualifications as U.S. trained nurses. Many state boards have established special training, citizenship, and experience requirements for students educated abroad, and others insist upon additional training in the United States. A few states have reciprocity or endorsement agreements with some foreign countries.

SUSPENSION AND REVOCATION

All nurse licensing boards have the authority to suspend or revoke the license of a nurse who is found in violation of specified norms of conduct. Such violations may include procurement of a license by fraud; unprofessional, dishonorable, immoral, or illegal conduct; performance of specific actions prohibited by the act; and malpractice.

Suspension and revocation procedures are most commonly contained in the licensing act; however, in some jurisdictions the procedure is left to the discretion of the board or is contained in general administrative procedure acts. For the most part, suspension and revocation proceedings are administrative rather than judicial and do not carry criminal sanctions. However, minimum due process standards must be maintained. These include (1) notifying the nurse of the charges, with enough certainty and definiteness so the nurse is able to prepare a defense, and (2) holding a hearing at which the nurse is permitted to present evidence. The hearing does not have to conform with full judicial hearings, but the final order must spell out the grounds for any action taken.

Several states have a great number and variety of grounds for revoking a nurse's license to practice. For example, revocation of license has been warranted when a nurse removed drugs from the employer's supply without authorization or for an unauthorized use and when a nurse interfered in matters concerning the treatment of patients which tended to promote friction between physicians and their patients.

Some licensing acts specifically authorize judicial review of board proceedings. This right may be limited to a review of the fairness and legality of the board action or it may permit a complete new trial, depending on the jurisdiction. The legislation typically designates which state court will hear the matter. The right to a judicial review of board proceedings is presumed in states whose nurse licensing acts do not provide specifically for it. The appropriate court is usually the lowest court of general jurisdiction. In either case, the general rule is that all administrative appeals must be exhausted before resorting to the courts.

LIABILITY FOR PRACTICING WITHOUT A LICENSE

Failure to obtain a license to practice nursing does not in itself raise a presumption or inference of negligence, nor does it constitute negligence per se. A plaintiff must allege and prove injury resulting from the unlicensed practitioner's negligence or lack of skill. The standard of care and skill used is the same one prevailing among properly licensed nurses. However, a patient may delay proper treatment, and be harmed by the delay, because of reliance upon the diagnosis and treatment of an unlicensed nurse. Such a showing may be sufficient to establish proximate cause for the injury, even though the unlicensed nurse's treatment itself may not have caused any injury. Insofar as a hospital's secondary liability is concerned, the general considerations of the doctrine of *respondeat superior* seem to apply. The mere fact that an unlicensed practitioner was hired and utilized by a hospital would not itself impose additional liability. Rather, an injured patient would still have to prove that the person allegedly responsible for the harm had in fact been negligent.

Section 2

DEFINITION OF NURSING PRACTICE

Nursing practice laws differ in their definitions of nursing practice. Whether a particular procedure in patient care falls within nursing practice or within medical practice is often a difficult question to answer, especially where licensing laws contain only a general definition of nursing practice. Physicians, hospitals, and other employers of nurses need authoritative and reliable guidelines. From time to time, nurses as well as their employers need to know whether a contemplated activity or procedure is within the scope of nursing practice. Yet there may be no way of obtaining an authoritative answer that eliminates the risk of a suit against a nurse for infringing upon the practice of physicians.

COMPULSORY AND VOLUNTARY ACTS

The trend in health occupation licensing has been toward compulsory licensing acts which permit only licensed personnel to practice the regulated occupation; unlicensed persons are prohibited from practicing in the field. This form of mandatory licensing can be contrasted with the system of voluntary licensing which permits only licensed personnel to use a particular title or designation, but does not prohibit unlicensed persons from working in the field. The only restriction on unlicensed persons under voluntary licensing is that they may not use the protected title. Often health fields are initially controlled by voluntary licensing requirements which eventually become compulsory.

In applying this distinction to nursing laws, mandatory nursing statutes forbid unlicensed persons to practice nursing and require that a person performing nursing acts must have met all the requirements relating to education, experience, and examination.

Voluntary nursing acts simply forbid an unlicensed person to use the professional title or to claim to be licensed. An example of a voluntary nursing statute is that of the *District of Columbia:*

> §2-401 REGISTRATION REQUIRED.
> No person shall in the District of Columbia in any manner whatsoever represent herself to be a registered, certified graduate, or trained nurse, or allow herself to be so represented, unless she has been and is registered or is registered by the Nurses' Examining Board in accordance with the provisions of this subchapter. . . .

> §2-410 NONREGISTERED NURSES MAY PRACTICE AS SUCH.
> Nothing in this subchapter shall be construed to prevent any person from nursing any other person in the District of Columbia, either gratuitously or for hire; *Provided,* That such person so nursing shall not represent herself as being a registered, certified, graduate, or trained nurse.

Not all health professionals are licensed in the same manner. State licensing regulations of such fields as medical practice, dentistry, chiropractic, pharmacy, optometry, podiatry, and osteopathy are always compulsory. In contrast, practitioners such as sanitarians, physical therapists, and social workers may be licensed under either compulsory or voluntary acts, depending on the jurisdiction. Professional associations which represent the practitioners in a particular field often seek actively to have compulsory licensing legislation enacted for their professions in order to upgrade their professional status and to improve the quality of care rendered by members of the profession.

NURSING PRACTICE DEFINED BY STATE LAW

Each state defines nursing differently. Some states define "the practice of nursing" in their licensing legislation, others define the "practice of professional nursing," and still others define "registered nurse" by outlining the duties that may be carried out by a registered nurse. The same range is also evident in the definition of "practical nurse" by each state.

The difficulty in defining nursing practice is attributable to the necessary distinction between medicine and nursing, as well as between professional and practical nursing. An example of a statute that distinguishes professional and practical nursing is that of *Rhode Island:*

* * * *

§5-34-1 DEFINITION OF TERMS. — As used in this Chapter:

* * * *

(d) Practice of Nursing:

(1) A person practices professional nursing, who, for compensation or personal profit, performs professional services requiring the application of the principles of nursing based on biological, physical, and social sciences, and nursing skills in the observation of symptoms, reactions, and accurate recording of facts, and carrying out of treatments and medications prescribed by licensed physicians in the care of the sick, in the prevention of disease or in the conservation of health.

(2) A person practices practical nursing, who, for compensation or personal profit, performs such duties as are required in the nursing care of subacute, convalescent or chronic patients, and in assisting the professional nurse in a team relationship, especially in the care of the more acutely ill and in carrying out medical orders as prescribed by a licensed physician, requiring a knowledge of simple nursing procedures but not requiring the knowledge and skills required for professional nursing.

The *Pennsylvania* nursing statute is an example of a law which does not prohibit others from performing certain "nursing" acts.

§214. PRACTICE OF MEDICINE NOT AUTHORIZED; ACTS NOT PROHIBITED.

This act confers no authority to practice medicine or surgery, nor does it prohibit—

(1) Services rendered by practical nurses, or home care of the sick by friends, domestic servants, nursemaids, companies or household aides of any type, so long as such persons do not represent or hold themselves out to be licensed nurses, licensed

registered nurses, or registered nurses; or use in connection with their names, any designation tending to imply that they are licensed to practice under the provision of this act.

(2) Gratuitous care of the sick by friends or members of the family.

(3) Domestic administration of family remedies by any person.

(4) Nursing services by anyone in case of an immediate emergency.

(5) Nursing by a person temporarily in this State, in compliance with an engagement made outside of this State, which engagement requires that such person accompany and care for a patient while temporarily in this State: Provided, however, That said engagement shall not be of more than six (6) months' duration.

(6) Care of the sick, with or without compensation or personal profit, when done in connection with the practice of the religious tenets of any church by adherents thereof.

(7) Auxiliary services rendered by persons carrying out duties necessary for the support of nursing service, including those duties which involve minor nursing services for patients, performed in hospitals or elsewhere under the direction of licensed physicians or supervision of licensed registered nurses.

(8) Nursing services rendered by a student enrolled in an approved school of nursing, when these services are a part of the course of study.

(9) Nursing services rendered by a graduate of an approved school of nursing in *Pennsylvania* or any other state, working under qualified supervision, during the period not to exceed one (1) year between completion of his or her course of nursing education and notification of the results of the licensing examination taken by such person, and during such additional period as the Board may in each case especially permit.

(10) Nursing services rendered by a person who holds a current license or other evidence of the right to practice professional nursing, as that term is defined in this act, issued by any other state, territory or province of the *United States* or the *Dominion of Canada,* during the period that an application filed by such person for licensure in *Pennsylvania* is pending before the Board, or for a period of one (1) year, whichever period first expires.

(11) The practice of professional nursing, within the definition of this act, by any person lawfully qualified so to practice in another state, territory, province or country, when such person is engaged in the practice of nursing as an employee of the *United States,* or by a person who is a foreign graduate nurse in the *United States* on nonimmigration status while enrolled in an approved, organized program of study as hereinafter provided.

Generally, each state provides certain standards of performance, knowledge, functions, and results in their legislative definitions of professional and practical nursing. The legal differences between professional and practical nursing are summarized as follows:

	Professional Nursing	Practical Nursing
Performance	Professional services	Duties required in nursing of sub-acute, convalescent or chronic patients
Required knowledge	Biological sciences Physical sciences Social sciences Nursing skills	Simple nursing procedures
Functions	Observe symptoms, record facts accurately, carry out treatments and medications prescribed by physician	Assist professional nurse (1) in care of acutely ill and (2) in carrying out medical orders prescribed by physician
Result of activity	Care of the sick, prevention of disease, conservation of health	Nursing subacute, convalescent or chronic patients

NURSING PRACTICE DEFINED BY THE A.N.A.

The American Nurses' Association provides the following model definitions of professional and practical nursing:

The term "practice of professional nursing" means the performance, for compensation, of any acts in the observation, care, and counsel of the ill, injured, or infirm or in the maintenance of health or prevention of illness of others, or in the supervision and teaching of other personnel, or the administration of medications and treatments as prescribed by a licensed physician or a licensed dentist; requiring substantial specialized judgment and skill and based on knowledge and application of the principles of biological, physical, and social science. The foregoing shall not be deemed to include acts of diagnosis or prescription of therapeutic or corrective measures.

The term "practical nursing" means the performance, for compensation, of selected acts in the care of the ill, injured, or infirm under the direction of a licensed professional nurse or a licensed physician or a licensed dentist; and not requiring the substantial specialized skill, judgment, and knowledge required in professional nursing.

The A.N.A. definitions are similar to those in certain states. However, in states which do not make a clear distinction between professional and practical nursing, the A.N.A. definitions provide reasonable guidelines for nurses.

MEDICAL PRACTICE DEFINED BY STATE LAW

Despite the fact that state laws vary in their definitions of what constitutes nursing practice, every state does clearly define the components of medical practice. Each state has enacted a medical practice act that permits those individuals who meet the necessary qualifications to use the Medical Doctor (M.D.) title and to practice medicine.

Essentially, the practice of medicine includes three functions: diagnosis, treatment, and prescription. A physician's license demonstrates that the state, as the representative of the public, has confidence that the physician has the training, experience, and ability to make diagnostic judgments, indicate courses of treatment, and specify medications, instruments, or procedures which will alleviate or cure a patient's ailment. Although medical personnel other than a physician may actually carry out medical techniques and procedures at the physician's direction or supervision, the physician's authority to make the necessary medical judgments is in no way impaired. Indeed, one primary judgment a physician must undertake is to determine what duties are to be carried out by either professional or practical nurses.

For example, a duly licensed and trained nurse who administers anesthetics under the personal direction and supervision of a licensed physician and surgeon is not engaging in the practice of medicine within the meaning of a licensing statute, although that service is usually performed by a physician; but the relation between the two professions is obvious.

Although a physician may perform all medical acts and is granted unlimited medical authority by virtue of state medical practice acts, hospitals may limit the medical procedures that a physician may actually perform. A hospital may require that before being permitted to perform certain medical procedures and before being certified by a specialty board, the physician must pass certain tests or engage in extra study and practice. For example, a physician may not be recognized as a psychiatrist until years are spent in special training. In any event, the state medical practice acts authorize a licensed physician—an individual permitted to use the title M.D.—to perform any act in the entire range of health services. No other health professional has that authorization.

Section 3
SCOPE OF PRACTICE ISSUES

A matter of considerable concern to many professional nurses is whether some of their patient care activities infringe upon the area of practice reserved by state licensing legislation to physicians only. The question can arise in almost any patient care setting, but it has been raised most frequently in regard to the emergency room and special care units, such as the coronary care unit. A nurse may believe that the assigned duties and functions imply that the nurse is being called upon to make medical diagnoses and select therapeutic measures, which are basic elements of medical practice. However, a nurse who engages in activities beyond the legally recognized scope of practice runs the risk of prosecution for violating the state medical practice act, and the hospital that employs the nurse could also be held criminally responsible for aiding and abetting the illegal practice of medicine.

In addition to the risk of criminal prosecution, the risk of civil liability for harm suffered by a patient may be enhanced in a suit alleging negligence if the nurse has exceeded the legal scope of nursing. The law in some states would allow a jury to infer that a nurse was negligent if the nurse performed functions restricted by law to physicians and harm was suffered by a patient. The burden then shifts to the nurse, who must establish that the performance was not of a negligent character. Even where such an inference is not recognized, the patient's attorney has the opportunity to put the nurse's performance in an unfavorable light if the facts suggest an intrusion into medical practice.

However, to put scope of practice in its proper perspective, it must be recognized that diagnosis and selection of therapeutic measures are matters of judgment. What is critical in assessing scope of practice questions related to nursing and medical practice is the determination of the nature and range of judgment assigned to the nurse. The nurse, who follows medically established guidelines applicable to fact situations and is qualified to recognize these situations is not engaging in the illegal practice of medicine. A nurse carrying out medical "standing orders," in a situation in which the nurse is allowed to determine whether specified conditions exist, thus indicating the need to execute the orders, is generally recognized as functioning within professional nursing practice.

Because of their concern over scope of practice issues professional organizations have developed practice statements clarifying rules and regulations of state medical and nursing boards, opinions of state attorneys general, and changes in licensing legislation, particularly nursing practice acts. The effect has been to broaden the range of activity for professional nurses within the law by eliminating some of the prior emphasis on maintaining an artificial division between medical practice and nursing practice. The trend is clearly toward greater flexibility in assigning responsibilities to nurses, The focus is on the individual nurse's competence, in light of education and experience, to fulfill the responsibilities without increased risk to patients, rather than on interpretating the definitions of practice in licensing legislation.

THE NURSE AS AN EMPLOYEE

WHEN A NURSE IS EMPLOYED BY A HOSPITAL, THE HOSPITAL ASSUMES responsibility for the nurse's work because the nurse is acting for the hospital in providing health care. The nurse can be thought of as representing the hospital. The hospital moreover assumes responsibility for a nurse's negligent actions, and in a case of liability it will be held liable along with the nurse.

Occasionally, a physician assumes responsibility for a nurse's actions, and if a nurse is negligent while acting under the physician's direct supervision, the physician will be held negligent.

Section 1

HOSPITAL LIABILITY—RESPONDEAT SUPERIOR

Respondeat superior is the term for a form of vicarious liability wherein an employer is held liable for the wrongful acts of an employee even though the employer's conduct is without fault. Liability predicated on *respondeat superior* may be imposed upon an employer only if a master-servant relationship exists between the employer and employee and if the wrongful act of the employee occur within the scope of employment. The test for determining whether a master-servant relationship sufficient to invoke the doctrine of *respondeat superior* exists is whether the employer has the right to control the physical conduct of the employee's performance of duties. An act "within the scope of employment" is so closely related to what the employee has been hired to do or so fairly and reasonably incidental to employment that it may be regarded as a method, although improper, of carrying out the orders of the employer.

The doctrine of *respondeat superior* does not absolve the employee of liability for wrongful acts. Not only may the injured party sue the employee directly, but the employer may also seek indemnification from the employee—that is, compensation for the financial loss occasioned by the employee's wrongful act. Since the employee is primarily responsible for the loss, the law does not relieve the employee of liability when the hospital is held liable through the application of *respondeat superior*.

In the instance of wrongful conduct by an independent contractor, the doctrine of *respondeat superior* does not apply. An independent contractor is usually an agent of a principal, over whom the principal has no right of control as to the manner in which the work is to be performed. The lack of the right of control over the agent makes the enterprise that of the independent contractor, rather than that of the principal.

The doctrine of *respondeat superior* may impose liability upon a hospital for a nurse's acts or omissions that result in injury to a hospital patient. Whether such liability attaches depends upon whether the conduct of the nurse was wrongful and whether the nurse was subject to the control of the hospital at the time the act in question was performed. The determination of whether the conduct of the nurse was wrongful in a given situation depends upon the standard of conduct to which the nurse is expected to adhere. The nurse who is subject to the control of the hospital at the time of the negligent conduct is considered an employee of the hospital and is not the "borrowed servant" of a staff physician or surgeon for liability purposes.

It is impossible to list all the acts and omissions which may constitute negligence on the part of a nurse and may render a hospital liable under the doctrine of *respondeat superior*. But some examples may illustrate the circumstances under which the doctrine will apply. Cases have involved the application of overheated hot water bottles, the administration of an enema of too high a temperature, the injection of incorrect medication, the failure to catheterize a patient at the intervals requested by the patient's physician, and the failure to warn a patient of the danger inherent in lowering a bed.

Likewise, a hospital will be held liable if a nurse continues to inject a solution after noticing its ill effects. For example, in the *Florida* case of *Parrish v. Clark*, [107 Fla. 598, 145 So. 848 (1933)], the court held that a nurse's continued injection of saline solution into an unconscious patient's breast after noticing ill effects constituted negligence. Thus, once something was observed to be wrong with the administration of the solution, the nurse had the duty to stop giving the solution.

A hospital will also be held liable for the failure of nursing personnel to take action when a patient's personal physician is clearly unwilling or unable to cope with a situation that threatens the life or health of the patient. In a *California* case, *Goff v. Doctors General Hospital*, [166 Cal. App. 2d 314, 333 P. 2d 29 (1958)], a patient was believed by two hospital nurses to be bleeding to death after childbirth because the physician failed to suture her properly. The nurses testified that they were aware of the patient's dangerous condition and that the physician was not present in the hospital. Both nurses knew the patient would die if nothing was done, but neither contacted anyone except the physician. The court held the hospital liable for the nurses' negligence in failing to notify the supervisors of the patient's serious condition, which caused the patient's death.

When a nurse deviates from the orders of the attending physician and the patient suffers injury thereby, a hospital may incur liability under the doctrine of *respondeat superior.* If the physician's therapeutic regimen for a patient is medically sound, it does not matter that the deviation from orders might be considered acceptable practice by other physicians or institutions.

Section 2

PHYSICIAN LIABILITY—"BORROWED SERVANT"

The "borrowed servant" doctrine is a special application of the doctrine of *respondeat superior* and applies when an employer lends an employee to another for a particular employment. Although the employee remains the servant of the employer, under the borrowed servant doctrine the regular employer is not liable for injury negligently caused by the servant while in the special service of another.

The borrowed servant rule provides that in certain situations, a nurse employed by a hospital may be considered the employee of the physician. In these situations, the physician is the special or temporary employer and is liable for the negligence of the nurse. To determine whether the physician is liable under *respondeat superior,* the plaintiff must establish that the physician had the right to control and direct the nurse at the time of the negligent act. If the physician is proved to be in exclusive control, and the nurse is deemed to be the physician's temporary special employee, the hospital is not liable for the nurse's negligent acts.

Inasmuch as the borrowed servant doctrine usually arises in a hospital within the context of the operating room, the application of this doctrine is based on acceptance of the "captain of the ship" concept, which views the surgeon as in total command of the operating room. The rationale for this concept was provided in the *Minnesota* case of *St. Paul-Mercury Indemnity Co. v. St. Joseph Hospital,* [212 Minn. 558, 4 N.W. 2d 637 (1942)], when the court stated:

> The desirability of the rule is obvious. The patient is completely at the mercy of the surgeon and relies upon him to see that all the acts relative to the operation are performed in a careful manner.

It is the surgeon's duty to guard against any and all avoidable
acts that may result in injury to his patient.

* * * *

The rule is plain that when the general employer assigns his
servant to duty for another and surrenders to the other direction
and control in relation to the work to be done, the servant
becomes the servant of the other insofar as his services relate to
the work so controlled and directed. His general employer is no
longer liable for the servant's torts committed in the directed and
controlled work. In the operating room the surgeon must be
master. He cannot tolerate any other voice in the control of his
assistants. In the case at bar the evidence is clear that the doctor
had exclusive control over the acts in question, and therefore the
hospital cannot be said to have been a "joint master" or
"comaster," even though the nurses were in its general employ
and paid by it.

Several courts have developed a distinction between a nurse's clerical or
administrative acts and those involving professional skill and judgment,
which are considered medical acts. The courts use this distinction in allo-
cating liability for the acts of a nurse as between the surgeon and the
hospital. If an act is characterized as adminstrative or clerical, it is the
hospital's responsibility; if the act is considered to be medical, it is the
surgeon's responsibility. This rule was enunciated in the *Minnesota* case of
Swigerd v. City of Ortonville, [246 Minn. 339, 75 N.W. 2d 217 (1956)],
when the court stated:

A hospital is liable for the negligence of its nurses in performing
mere administrative or clerical acts, which acts, *though constituting a part of patient's prescribed medical treatment,* do not
require the application of the specialized technique or the
understanding of a skilled physician or surgeon. This rule, in
recognizing that the right of control remains with the hospital as
the general employer, is consistent with the nature of such acts
and is in accord with the custom which in everyday practice
governs the relationship between the hospital staff and the attending physicians. It is generally recognized that the nature of
the acts performed, and the custom as to the control ordinarily
exercised in the performance of similar acts, are factors indica-
tive of where the right control exists.

As to what acts may be properly labeled administrative, the *Swigerd* court
noted further:

No all-embracing definition of what acts are administrative will
be attempted but a few illustrations from actual cases will suffice
to disclose their nature. It has been held that the order of an at-

tending physician that sideboards be placed on a bed for the patient's protection is a medical determination for which the hospital is not responsible. In contrast, however, the physical or manual act of attaching the sideboards, in compliance with that order, is merely an administrative act since it can be performed by anyone in the hospital's employ and its performance requires no professional knowledge, skill, or experience. Similarly, where a doctor ordered that his patient be served tea, the negligent serving of the tea, whereby the patient was painfully burned, was an administrative act for which the hospital was liable in damages.

Although the distinction between administrative and other acts is occasionally stated by courts in order to determine whether the hospital or the physician is liable for a nurse's negligent acts, in *New York* where this distinction was first advanced and in many other jurisdictions it is regarded as lacking in sound judgment.

Section 3

SPECIAL DUTY NURSE

The hospital is usually not held liable for the negligence of a special duty nurse—a nurse hired by the patient or the patient's family to perform nursing services. Generally, the relationship of master and servant does not exist between the hospital and the special duty nurse.

In some respects a special nurse might be likened to a staff physician. Thus a hospital may exclude a special nurse from practicing within the institution. As with staff physicians, a special nurse may be required to observe the rules as a precondition to working in the hospital. The observance of hospital rules is insufficient, however, to raise a master-servant relationship between the hospital and the nurse. Under ordinary circumstances a special nurse is employed by the patient; the hospital has no authority to hire or fire or to control the nurse's conduct on the case, but retains responsibility to protect patients from incompetent and unqualified special nurses.

Even though a special nurse is employed by the patient, the hospital may be held liable if the nurse is negligent in performing administrative duties required by the hospital. Moreover, use of the designation "special nurse" does not preclude consideration of the nurse as an employee or agent of the hospital. If a master-servant relationship exists between the hospital and the special nurse, the doctrine of *respondeat superior* may be applied to impose liability upon the hospital for the nurse's wrongful conduct. Thus in *Emory University v. Shadburn*, [47 Ga. App. 643, 171 S.E. 192 (1933)], the court, emphasizing that the nurse was procured and paid through the hospital, stated:

Where an application in behalf of the patient is made to the hospital to furnish to the patient a special nurse, and a special nurse is selected and procured by the hospital and placed in charge of the patient, notwithstanding the services of the nurse may be specifically charged for by the hospital and paid for by the patient, but where the hospital itself is paid for the services of the nurse and the hospital afterwards settles with the nurse, the inference is authorized that the special nurse is the agent of the hospital to care for and look after the patient; and where the injuries received by the patient in jumping out of the window of the hospital under the conditions referred to are caused from any negligence of the nurse in leaving the patient alone, such negligence is imputable to the hospital.

Thus even though a patient pays the special nurse, the existence of an employer-employee relationship, which determines the applicability of *respondeat superior,* is a matter of fact to be determined by the jury under proper instructions.

Section 4
SUPERVISING NURSE

A supervising nurse is not liable under *respondeat superior* for the negligent acts of the nurses being supervised. The supervising nurse has the right to direct the nurses who are being supervised; but the hospital is the employer, and the supervisory powers flow directly from the hospital's right of control. However, the supervisory nurse is liable for personal negligent behavior, and the hospital may be liable for the negligent acts of all employees, including supervisors.

For example, in the case of *Bowers v. Olch,* [120 Cal. 2d 108, 260 P. 2d 997 (1953)], a supervising nurse assigned two nurses to an operating room. One of the nurses left a needle in a patient's abdomen after an operation. The patient charged that the supervising nurse was liable under the doctrine of *respondeat superior* because she assigned the nurse to the operating room. The court dismissed the case against the supervising nurse and stated that the doctrine of *respondeat superior* did not apply because the supervising nurse could not exercise control over the conduct of the nurses.

LABOR

MANY FEDERAL AND STATE LAWS REGULATE THE RELATIONSHIP BETWEEN employers and employees. Some of these laws are pertinent to the relationship between hospitals and nurses. Such laws cover the areas of union activity and employment practices, including wages, hours, child labor laws, and workmen's compensation.

Section 1
UNIONS AND HOSPITALS

The nurse who is employed by a hospital is likely to be more concerned with labor relations than a nurse who is privately employed. Furthermore, the nurse's concern will be much greater today than it was ten years ago. Unions have only recently become a large factor in hospital-employee relations. Until the mid-1930s, union organizational activity in hospitals was minimal, and until the late 1950s it increased relatively slowly. However, in the past 15 years unions have begun to play a considerably greater part in hospital-employee relations.

A number of different labor organizations are now heavily involved in attempts to become the recognized collective bargaining representatives in the hospital field. There are craft unions whose primary organizing efforts are devoted to skilled employees, such as carpenters and electricians; industrial unions and unions of governmental employees, which seek to represent large groups of unskilled or semiskilled employees; and professional and occupational associations and societies, such as state nurses' associations, which are interested in representing their members. To the extent that the professional organizations seek goals directly concerned with wages, hours, and other employment conditions and engage in bargaining on behalf of employees, they perform the functions of labor unions.

69

Union activity in the hospital field has generally been successful in the geographical areas where unions have been successful in other industries. It is not unreasonable to assume that this pattern will continue.

Section 2
FEDERAL LABOR ACTS

LABOR-MANAGEMENT RELATIONS ACT

The Labor-Management Relations Act (LMRA) defines certain conduct of employers and employees as unfair labor practices and provides for hearings upon complaints that such practices have occurred. This Act consists of the National Labor Relations Act of 1935, the Taft-Hartley amendments of 1947, and certain amendments contained in the Labor-Management Reporting and Disclosure Act of 1959.

Jurisdiction. Nearly all proprietary hospitals have for some time, been subject to the provisions of the Labor-Management Relations Act. The National Labor Relations Board (NLRB), which is entrusted with enforcing and administering the Act, has jurisdiction over matters involving proprietary hospitals with gross revenues of at least $250,000 per year.

An exemption of governmental hospitals was included in the 1935 enactment of the National Labor Relations Act, and charitable hospitals were exempted in 1947 by judicial decision. However, a July 1974 amendment to the National Labor Relations Act extended coverage to employees of nonprofit health care institutions that had previously been exempted from its provisions. In the words of the amendment, a health care facility is "any hospital, convalescent hospital, health maintenance organization, health clinic, nursing home, extended care facility, or other institution devoted to the care of the sick, infirm or aged."

The amendment also enacted unique special provisions for employees of health care facilities who oppose unionization on legitimate religious grounds. These provisions allow a member of such an institution to make periodic contributions to one of three nonreligious charitable funds selected jointly by the labor organization and the employing institution, rather than pay periodic union dues and initiation fees. If the collective bargaining agreement does not specify an acceptable fund, the employee may select a tax-exempt charity.

Elections. The LMRA sets out the procedures by which employees may select a labor organization as their collective bargaining representative to negotiate with the hospital over employment and contract matters. A hospital may choose to recognize and deal with the union without resorting to the formal LMRA procedure. If the formal process is adhered to, the employees vote on union representation in an election held under NLRB supervision. If the union wins, it is certified by the NLRB as the employees' bargaining representative.

The LMRA provides that the representatives having been selected by a majority of employees in a bargaining unit is the exclusive bargaining agent for *all* employees in the unit. The scope of the bargaining unit is often the subject of dispute, for these boundaries may determine the outcome of the election, the employee representative's bargaining power, and the level of labor relations stability.

When the parties cannot agree on the appropriate unit for bargaining, the NLRB has broad discretion to decide the issue. But the NLRB's discretion is limited to determining appropriate units from only those employees who are classified as professional, supervisory, clerical, technical, or service and maintenance employees and are to be included in units outside of their particular category. This is the case unless there has been a self-determination election, in which the members of a certain group vote, as a class, to be included within the larger bargaining unit. For example, nurses and other professional employees of a hospital can be excluded from a bargaining unit composed of service and maintenance employees, unless the professionals are first given the opportunity to choose separate representation and reject it. Supervisory nurses have also been held to be entitled to a bargaining unit separate from the unit composed of general duty nurses.

While the LMRA does not require the employee representatives to be selected by any particular procedure, the Act provides for the NLRB to conduct representation elections by secret ballot. The NLRB may only conduct such an election when a petition for certification has been filed by an employee, a group of employees, an individual, a labor union acting on the employees' behalf, or an employer. When the petition is filed the NLRB must investigate and must direct an election if it has reasonable cause to believe a question of representation exists. After an election, if any party to it believes that the election was accompanied by conduct creating an atmosphere that interfered with employee free choice, that party may file objections with the NLRB.

Unfair Labor Practices. Labor-Management Relations Act prohibits hospitals from engaging in certain conduct classified as employer unfair labor practices. For example, firing an employee for holding union membership is not permitted. The LMRA stipulates that the employer must bargain in good faith with representatives of the employees, and failure to do so constitutes an unfair labor practice. The NLRB may order the employer to fulfill the duty to bargain.

If the employer dominates or controls the employees' union, or interferes and supports one of two competing unions, the employer is committing an unfair labor practice. Such employer support of a competing union is clearly illustrated in a situation in which two unions are competing for members in the hospital, as well as for recognition as the organization to bargain on behalf of the employees. If the hospital permits one of the unions to use hospital facilities for its organizational activities, but denies the use of the facilities to the other union, an unfair labor practice is committed. Financial assistance to one of the competing unions also constitutes an unfair labor practice.

The LMRA also places duties on labor organizations and prohibits certain employee activities that are denominated as employee unfair labor practices. Coercion of employees by the union constitutes an unfair labor practice; and activities such as mass picketing, assaults on nonstrikers, and following groups of nonstrikers away from the immediate area of the hospital plainly constitute coercion and will be ordered stopped by the NLRB. Breach of a collective bargaining contract by the labor union is another example of a union unfair labor practice.

Labor Disputes. Congress enacted the Norris-LaGuardia Act to limit the power of the federal courts to issue injunctions in cases involving or growing out of labor disputes. The Act's strict standards must be met before such injunctions can be issued. Essentially, a federal court may not apply restraints in a labor dispute except after the case is heard in open court and the finding is that unlawful acts will be committed unless restrained and that substantial and irreparable injury to the complainant's property will follow.

The Norris-LaGuardia Act is aimed at reducing the number of injunctions granted to restrain strikes and picketing. An additional piece of legislation setting out procedures limiting strikes in health institutions is the 1974 amendment to the National Labor Relations Act.

This amendment sets out special procedures for handling labor disputes developing out of collective bargaining at the termination of an existing agreement or during negotiations for an initial contract between a health institution and its employees. The procedures were designed to ensure that the needs of patients would be met during any work stoppage (strike) or labor dispute in such an institution.

The amendment provides for creating a board of inquiry if a dispute threatens to interrupt health care in a particular community. The board is appointed by the director of the Federal Mediation and Conciliation Service (FMCS) within 30 days after notification of either party's intention to terminate a labor contract. The board then has 15 days in which to investigate and report its findings and recommendations. Once the report is filed with the FMCS, both parties are expected to maintain the status quo for an additional 15 days.

The board's findings are to provide a framework for arbitrators' decisions, while recognizing both the community's need for continuous health services and the good-faith intentions of labor organizations to avoid a work stoppage whenever possible and to accept arbitration when negotiations reach an impasse.

The amendment also mandates certain notice requirements by labor groups in health care institutions. First, 90-days' notice must be given to the institution before a collective bargaining agreement expires, and the Federal Mediation and Conciliation Service is entitled to 60-days' notice. Previously, 60-days' notice to the employer and 30-days' notice to the FMCS was all that was required. However, if the bargaining agreement is the initial contract between the parties, only 30-days' notice need be given to the FMCS.

More significantly, 10-days' notice is required in advance of any strike, picketing, or other concerted refusal to work, regardless of the source of the dispute. This allows the NLRB to determine the legality of a strike before it occurs and also gives health care institutions ample time to ensure the continuity of patient treatment. At the same time, any attempt to utilize this period to undermine the bargaining relationship is implicitly forbidden.

The 10-day notice may be concurrent with the final 10 days of the expiration notice. Any employee violation of these provisions amounts to an unfair labor practice and may automatically result in the discharge of the employee. In addition, injunctive relief may be available from the courts if circumstances warrant.

In summary, the amendment's provisions are designed to ensure that every possible approach to a peaceful settlement is fully explored before a strike is called in hospitals and other healthcare facilities.

LABOR-MANAGEMENT REPORTING AND DISCLOSURE ACT

The Labor-Management Reporting and Disclosure Act of 1959 places controls upon labor unions and the relationships between unions and their members. In addition, it requires that employers report payments and loans to officials or other representatives of labor organizations or any promises to make such payments or loans. Payments to employees for the purpose of influencing the way they exercise their rights to organize and bargain collectively are illegal unless the employer at the same time discloses such payments. Expenditures with the object of interfering with employee rights to organize and bargain collectively must also be disclosed, as well as agreements with labor relations consultants under which such persons undertake to interfere with certain employee rights.

Reports required under this law must be filed with the Secretary of Labor and are then made public. Both charitable and proprietary hospitals that make such payments or enter into such agreements must file the reports, but governmental hospitals are not subject to these provisions. Penalties for failure to make the required reports, or for making false reports, include fines to the extent of $10,000 and imprisonment for one year.

FAIR LABOR STANDARDS ACT

The Fair Labor Standards Act establishes minimum wages and maximum hours of employment. The employees of all governmental, charitable, and proprietary hospitals are covered by this Act, and hospitals must conform to the minimum wage and overtime pay provisions. However, bona fide executive, administrative, and professional employees are exempted from the wage and hour provisions.

The law permits hospitals to enter into agreements with employees, establishing an alternative work period of 14 consecutive days, rather than the usual seven-day week. If the alternative period is chosen, the hospital need pay the overtime rate only for any hours worked in excess of 80 hours during the 14-day period. It should be noted that the alternate fourteen-day work period does not relieve the hospital from paying overtime for hours worked in excess of 8 in any one day, even if no more than 80 hours are worked during the period.

EQUAL EMPLOYMENT OPPORTUNITY

Title VII of the Civil Rights Act of 1964 as amended by the Equal Employment Opportunity Act of 1972 prohibits private employers and state and local governments from discriminating on the basis of race, color, religion, sex, or national origin. An exception to prohibited employment practices may be permitted when religion, sex, or national origin is a bona fide occupational qualification necessary to the operation of a particular business or enterprise.

The act also exempts hospitals operated by religious corporations or societies, but only with respect to employees directly concerned with religious activities. It should be noted that practically all employment in hospitals operated by religious bodies is unrelated to religious activity.

Many states have enacted "protective" laws with respect to the employment of females. The EEOC guidelines on sex discrimination make it clear that state laws limiting the employment of females in certain occupations are superseded by Title VII and are no defense against a charge of sex discrimination.

Section 3
STATE LAWS

STATE LABOR-MANAGEMENT RELATIONS ACT

Because the LMRA excludes from coverage hospitals operated by the state or its political subdivisions, the regulation of labor-management relations in these hospitals is left to state law. State laws vary considerably in their coverage, and often employees of state and local governmental hospitals are covered by separate public employee legislation. Some of these statutes cover both state and local employees, whereas others cover only state or only local employees.

Most states have no labor relations statutes. Unless the constitution in those states guarantees the right of employees to organize and imposes the duty of collective bargaining on the employer, most hospitals would not have to bargain collectively with their employees. In states that do have labor relations acts, the obligation of a hospital to bargain collectively with its employees is determined by the applicable statute.

A number of states have statutes similar to the Norris-LaGuardia Act, restricting the granting of injunctions in labor disputes. There are anti-injunction acts in several other states which are different from this type, and decisions under them do not fall into an easily recognized pattern.

Of the states which have labor relations acts granting the employees of hospitals the right to organize, join unions, and bargain collectively, some states have specifically prohibited strikes and lockouts and have provided for compulsory arbitration whenever a collective bargaining contract cannot otherwise be executed amicably. Anti-injunction statutes would not forbid injunctions to restrain violations of these statutory provisions.

The courts have almost uniformly held that labor strife involving a charitable hospital does not constitute a labor dispute within the meaning of the anti-injunction acts. Where a proprietary hospital is involved, the courts may still decide that the anti-injunction act is inapplicable and may therefore grant an injunction. However, the determination would be based on the particular situation, rather than on any theory that all hospitals should be excluded.

It should be noted that the doctrine of federal preemption, as applied to labor relations, displaces the states' jurisdiction to regulate an activity that is arguably an unfair labor practice within the meaning of the LMRA. Despite the broad sweep of the doctrine of federal preemption, the U.S. Supreme Court has ruled that states can still regulate labor relations activity that also falls within the jurisdiction of the NLRB where deeply rooted local feelings and responsibility are affected. Thus violence, threats of violence, mass picketing, and obstructing streets may be regulated by the states.

UNION SECURITY CONTRACTS AND RIGHT-TO-WORK LAWS

Labor organizations frequently seek to enter into union security contracts with employers. Such contracts are of two types: the closed shop contract, which provides that only members of a particular union may be hired; and the union shop contract, which makes continued employment dependent upon membership in the union, although the employee need not have been a union member when applying for the job or being hired.

More than one-third of all the states have made such contracts unlawful. Statutes forbidding such agreements are generally called right-to-work laws on the theory that they protect everyone's right to work, even if he refuses to join a union. Several other state statutes or decisions purport to restrict union security contracts, or provide for procedures to be completed before such agreements may be made.

ANTI-DISCRIMINATION ACTS

State acts which prohibit discriminatory practices in employment are of little importance in light of the broad coverage of the federal equal employment opportunities provisions. All hospitals, except governmental hospitals, are employers under this federal statute and subject to its provisions. However, a few state statutes prohibit discrimination because of age, a prohibition not covered by federal legislation.

WAGE AND HOUR LAWS

State legislation establishing minimum wage rates is also of minor importance because the 1966 amendment to the federal Fair Labor Standards Act, provides that hospital personnel be covered by the Act. Where state minimum wage standards are higher than federal standards, the state's standards are applicable to hospital employees.

CHILD LABOR ACTS

Many states prohibit the employment of minors below a certain age and restrict the employment of other minors. Child labor legislation commonly requires that working papers be secured before a child may be hired, forbids the employment of minors at night, and provides that minors may not operate certain types of dangerous machinery.

This kind of legislation rarely exempts charitable hospitals, although some exceptions may be made with respect to the hours when student nurses may work.

REGULATION OF EMPLOYEE OCCUPATIONAL HEALTH AND SAFETY

Congress enacted the Occupational Safety and Health Act of 1970 to establish administrative machinery for the development and enforcement of standards for occupational health and safety. Standards developed for various industries will be mandatory for all covered employers. There are at present no standards for the health care industry. The statute provides that where no federal standard has been established, state safety rules will remain in effect.

Under the law of some states, employers are charged with the duty of furnishing employees with a safe place to work. Of course, even in the absence of such statutes, a hospital would be liable if employees were injured because of negligence in the care of the premises or the upkeep of equipment unless the doctrine of charitable or governmental immunity were applicable or unless the employees were covered by workmen's compensation.

In addition to provisions relating to safety, other state statutes require that certain facilities—lavatories, for example, and seats for elevator operators—be provided for the employees. The city and county in which a hospital is located may also prescribe rules regarding the health and safety of employees. Many communities have enacted sanitary and health codes that require certain facilities or standards, for example. It should be emphasized that in most instances convenience and safety laws do not exempt charitable institutions.

WORKMEN'S COMPENSATION

An employee who is injured while performing job-related duties may sue the employer for injuries suffered. State legislatures have recognized that it is difficult and expensive for employees to recover from their employers and have therefore enacted workmen's compensation laws.

Workmen's compensation laws give the employee a legal way to receive compensation for injuries on the job. The acts do not require the employee to prove that the injury was the result of the employer's negligence. Workmen's compensation laws are based on the employer-employee relationship and not upon the theory of negligence.

The scope of workmen's compensation varies widely. Some states limit an employee's compensation to the amount recoverable by the workmen's compensation law, and further lawsuits against the employer are barred. Other states permit the employee to choose whether to accept the compensation provided by law or institute a lawsuit against the employer. Some acts go further and provide a system of insurance which may be under the supervision of state or private insurers. Recovery by an employee begins with a hearing on the claim before a board of commissioners. Following the hearing, the commissioners decide whether there was an employee-employer relationship, whether the injury is covered by the act, and whether there is a connection between the employment and the injury. The commissioners then award compensation according to a predetermined schedule based on the nature of the injury. Though the amount of compensation is generally not as high as might be received in a lawsuit for negligence, the employee is more likely to receive some compensation. Generally, workmen's compensation boards tend to be liberal in interpreting the law to provide compensation for employees.

INSURANCE

Today, almost everyone has some form of insurance. We insure our automobiles against collision and theft, and we take out fire insurance on our homes. We insure our personal property, ourselves, and the members of our family. Professional personnel also buy insurance to protect themselves from suit in the event that others are injured as a result of their professional services. What kinds of insurace are purchased depends on individual needs.

Section 1

DEFINITION

Insurance is a contract in which the insurer agrees to assume certain risks of the insured, in exchange for a premium. In the terms of the contract, also known as the insurance policy, the insurer promises to pay a specific amount of money if a specified event takes place. An insurance policy contains three necessary elements: (1) identification of the risk involved; (2) the specific amount payable; and (3) the specified occurrence.

A risk is the possibility that a loss will occur. The major function of insurance is to provide security against this loss. Insurance does not prevent or hinder the occurrence of the loss, but it does compensate for the damages.

There are three categories of risks to which an insured individual may be exposed: (1) risks of property loss or damage; (2) personal risks or loss of life; and (3) legal liability. Property risk is the possibility that an insured's property may be damaged or destroyed by fire, flood, tornado, hurricane, or other catastrophe. Personal risk is the possibility that the insured may be injured in an accident or may become ill; the possibility of death is a personal risk provided for in the typical life insurance plan. Legal liability risk is the possibility that the insured may become legally liable to pay money damages to another and includes accident and professional liability insurance.

Section 2
NURSING RISK

A nurse who provides professional services to another person for pay may be legally responsible for any harm that the person suffers as a result of the nurse's negligence; furthermore, the nurse may be subject to a loss of money in the form of legally awarded damages. Many nurses protect themselves from the risk of a legal loss by acquiring a professional liability insurance policy. A student nurse may also be legally liable for any harm that stems from nursing negligence. For this reason some student nurses obtain professional liability insurance, similar to the coverage for registered nurses, in order to be protected in the event of legal losses.

Section 3
PROFESSIONAL LIABILITY INSURANCE POLICY

A nurse who is covered by a professional liability insurance policy must recognize the rights and duties inherent in the policy. The nurse should be able to identify the risks that are covered, the amount of coverage, and the conditions of the contract.

Although coverage may vary in the policies of different insurance companies, the standard policy usually says the insurance company will "pay on behalf of the insured all sums which the insured shall become legally obligated to pay as damages because of injury arising out of malpractice, error, or mistake in rendering or failing to render nursing services."

A standard liability insurance policy has five distinct parts: (1) the insurance agreement; (2) defense and settlement; (3) policy period; (4) amount payable; and (5) conditions. [☞ For a sample policy, see Appendix C.]

Insurance Agreement

An insurance policy usually states that the insurer will pay on behalf of the insured all sums of money which the insured becomes legally liable to pay. The insurer, under the terms of the policy, has no obligation to pay any sum over and above the legal liability and will not pay a sum of money merely because the insured feels a moral obligation toward an injured party.

Under a professional liability policy, the nurse is protected from damages arising from rendering or failing to render nursing services. Thus a nurse who performs a negligent act resulting in legal liability is personally protected from paying an injured party. The actual payment of the legal money damages to the injured party is accomplished by the insurer. The nurse is also protected from damages resulting from acts which should have been performed, but were not.

DEFENSE AND SETTLEMENT

In the defense and settlement portion of the insurance policy, the nurse and the insurance company agree that the company will defend any lawsuit against the nurse arising from performance or nonperformance of nursing services, and that the company is delegated the power to effect a settlement of any claims as it deems necessary. A policy stating that the insurer will provide a defense of all lawsuits guarantees such a defense in any suit including those that are groundless, false, or fraudulent. In the case of a professional liability policy, the duty of the insurer under this clause is limited to the defense of lawsuits against the nurse which are a consequence of nursing services.

If an insurance company has established the right to obtain a settlement of any claim before trial, the company's only obligation is to act reasonably and not to the detriment of the insured.

POLICY PERIOD

The period of the policy is always stated in the insurance contract. The contract provides protection only for risks that occur during the time when the policy is stated to be effective. Thus any accident that occurred before or after the policy period would not be covered under the insuring agreement.

AMOUNT PAYABLE

The amount to be paid by the insurer is determined by the amount of damage suffered by the injured party. This determination may be made by a jury, or the insurance company and the injured party may reach a settlement before a lawsuit comes to trial or before the jury has determined the amount of damages. In any event, the insurance company will pay to the injured party no more than the maximum coverage stated in the insurance policy.

For example, if a jury determines that a nurse is liable to an injured person for $45,000, and the maximum coverage in the nurse's insurance policy is $40,000, the insurance company will pay only $40,000 to the injured party: the remaining $5,000 must be provided from other resources by the nurse.

A further example is the policy whose maximum coverage is $40,000 for each claim and $120,000 for aggregate claims. Under this policy, the aggregate claims figure is the total amount payable to all injured parties. Thus the insured is protected on each individual claim up to $40,000; when there is more than one claim, the insured is protected up to $40,000 on each of three claims. Should there be more than three claims, the aggregate $120,000 would be spread across all claims, but payment would not exceed $40,000 on any one claim.

CONDITIONS OF THE POLICY

Each insurance policy contains a number of important conditions, and failure to comply with these conditions may cause forfeiture of the policy and nonpayment of claims against it. Generally, insurance policies contain the following conditions: (1) notice of occurrence; (2) notice of claim; (3) assistance of the insured; (4) other insurance; (5) assignment; (6) subrogation; (7) changes; and (8) cancellation.

1. *Notice of occurrence.* When the insured becomes aware that an injury has occurred as a result of acts covered under the contract, the insured must promptly notify the insurance company. The form of notice may be either oral or written, as specified in the policy.

2. *Notice of claim.* Whenever the insured receives notice that a claim or suit is being instituted, notice must be sent by the insured to the insurance company. The policy will specify what papers are to be forwarded to the company.

3. *Assistance of the insured.* The insured must cooperate with the insurance company and render any assistance necessary to reach a settlement.

4. *Other insurance.* If the insured has pertinent insurance policies with other insurance companies, the insured must notify the insurance company in order that each company may pay the appropriate amount of the claim.

5. *Assignment.* The protections contracted for by the insured may not be transferred unless permission is granted by the insurance company. Because the insurance company was aware of the risks the insured would encounter before the policy was issued, the company will endeavor to avoid protecting persons other than the policy holder.

6. *Subrogation.* Subrogation is the right of a person who pays another's debt to be substituted for all rights in relation to the debt. When an insurance company makes a payment for the insured under the terms of the policy, the company becomes the beneficiary of all the rights of recovery the insured has against any other persons who may also have been negligent. For example, if several nurses were found liable for negligence arising out of the same occurrence, and the insurance company for one nurse pays the entire claim, the company will be substituted to the rights of that nurse and may collect a proportionate share of the claim from the other nurses.

7. *Changes.* The insured cannot make changes in the policy without the written consent of the insurance company. Thus an agent of the insurance company ordinarily cannot modify or remove any condition of the liability contract. Only the insurance company by written authorization may permit a condition to be altered or removed.

8. *Cancellation.* A cancellation clause spells out the conditions and procedures necessary for the insured or the insurer to cancel the liability policy. Written notice is usually required. The insured person's failure to comply with any of the conditions can result in nonpayment of a claim by the insurance company. An insurance policy is a contract, and failure to meet the terms and conditions of the contract may result in the penalties associated with breach of contract, such as nonpayment of claims.

Section 4
MEDICAL PROFESSIONAL LIABILITY INSURANCE

The fundamental tenets of insurance law and its application to the typical liability insurance policy are pertinent to the provisions of medical professional liability insurance as applied to individuals and institutions.

Professional liability policies vary in the broadness of the insuring clauses, the exclusions from coverage, and the interpretations a company places on the language of the contract.

There are three medical professional liability classes:

1. Individuals including (but not limited to) physicians, surgeons, dentists, nurses, osteopaths, chiropodists, chiropractors, opticians, physiotherapists, optometrists, and various types of medical technicians. This category may also include medical laboratories, blood blanks, and optical establishments.

2. Hospitals and related institutions such as extended care facilities, homes for the aged, institutions for the mentally ill, sanitariums, and other health institutions where bed and board are provided for patients or residents.

3. Clinics, dispensaries, and infirmaries where there are no regular bed or board facilities. These institutions may be related to industrial or commercial enterprises; however, they are to be distinguished from facilities operated by dentists or physicians, which are usually covered under individual professional liability contracts.

The insuring clause will usually provide for payment on behalf of the insured if an injury arises from —

1. Malpractice, error, or mistake in rendering or failing to render professional services in the practice of the insured's profession during the policy period.

2. Act or omissions on the part of the insured during the policy period as a member of a formal accreditation or similar professional board or committee of a hospital or a professional society.

The "injury" is not limited to bodily injury or property damage. However, the injury must result from malpractice, error, mistake, or the failure to perform acts that should have been performed.

The most common risks covered by medical professional liability insurance are negligence, assault and battery from failing to obtain consent to a medical or surgical procedure, libel and slander, and invasion of privacy for betrayal of professional confidences. Coverage varies from company to company because of differences in interpretation of the same or similar language. The premium rates for each state are generally established by the state legislature, and the rates differ for individuals, hospitals, and clinics.

PART III

THE NURSE AND SOCIETY

CIVIL RIGHTS

Civil rights are rights assured by the Constitution of the United States and by acts of Congress and state legislatures. Generally, the term includes all the rights of each individual in a free society. Nurses will be specifically interested in three major areas of law which deal with civil rights. First, the Civil Rights Act of 1964 contains provisions relating to hospitals. Second, the Hill-Burton Act defines certain requirements for hospitals receiving aid under its program. And third, some state laws deal with discriminatory admission policies in hospitals and other health facilities, which often directly involve nurses.

The nurse shares the hospital's legal responsibility in the enforcement of civil rights. In dealing with patients, visitors, and fellow employees, the nurse is prohibited from making discriminatory distinctions based on race, color, religion, sex, or national origin.

Section 1

DISCRIMINATION

Federal Regulations

Discriminatory practices in hospitals and other health facilities have been dealt with by Congress and the federal courts. Discrimination in admission of patients and segregation of patients on racial grounds is for all practical purposes proscribed in any hospital receiving federal financial assistance. Pursuant to Title VI of the Civil Rights Act of 1964, the guidelines of the Department of Health, Education and Welfare (H.E.W.) require that there be no racial discrimination practiced by any hospital or agency receiving money under any program supported by H.E.W. This includes all hospitals which are "providers of service" receiving federal funds under Medicare legislation.

According to the Fourteenth Amendment to the Constitution, a state cannot act so as to deny to any person equal protection of the laws. If a state or a political subdivision of a state, whether through its executive, judicial, or legislative branch, acts in such a way as to unfairly deny to one person the rights accorded to another, the Amendment has been violated. If the state supports or authorizes an activity for the benefit of the public, it is possible that a nongovernmental institution engaging in such activity will be considered to be engaged in state action and subject to the Fourteenth Amendment.

The acts of the executive, judicial, and legislative branches of government encompass the acts of government agencies as well, and "state action" has been extended to include activities of nongovernmental entities under certain circumstances.

Considering the constitutional requirements together with the H.E.W. guidelines and Title II of the Civil Rights Act of 1964, which prohibits discrimination in restaurants and other places of public accommodation and thus may include restaurants in hospitals, it is apparent that racial discrimination is prohibited in practically all hospitals.

The Civil Rights Act of 1964 is particularly important to the nurse because it provides that the hospital must treat the nurse, along with patients, physicians, and other employees, in a nondiscriminatory manner. Title VII makes it illegal to deny equal job opportunities on the basis of race, color, religion, sex, or national origin; it also prohibits the nurse, as an employee of the hospital, from discriminating against patients, physicians, or fellow employees.

STATE REGULATIONS

Most states have enacted laws to protect the civil rights of its citizens. Some of these statutes declare that life, liberty, and the pursuit of happiness should not be denied; others adhere closely to the language of federal civil rights legislation.

For example, the *Massachusetts* Civil Rights Act forbids discrimination in places of "public accommodation, resort or amusement" against persons who belong to any religious sect, creed, class, race, color, sex, denomination, or nationality. The statute defines the phrase "place of public accommodation, resort or amusement" to include hospitals, dispensaries, and clinics operating for profit. However, it excludes places owned or operated by any religious, racial, or denominational institution or organization, as well as any organization operated for charitable or educational purposes.

The *Pennsylvania* Human Relations Act is somewhat similar to the *Massachusetts* Act in that it specifically includes dispensaries, clinics, and hospitals within its definition of public accommodation, resort or amusement. But the *Pennsylvania* Act does not apply to distinctly private institutions.

Missouri's act is not as specific as either the *Pennsylvania* or *Massa-*

chusetts acts. It does not mention hospitals within its coverage. However, the phrase "places of public accommodation" would seem to include hospitals, since the definition includes all places or businesses offering services, facilities, and accommodations for the peace, comfort, health, welfare, and safety of the general public.

Some state laws still require separation of the races or other discriminatory practices in governmental and private institutions, including hospitals. The methods and manner of discrimination vary. Although these laws remain on the books, they are not valid; should they be attacked in the courts they would undoubtedly be ruled unconstitutional.

Section 2
HILL—BURTON ACT

The Hospital Survey and Construction Act, popularly known as the Hill-Burton Act, provides that any hospital receiving funds from this program must make available a reasonable number of services to persons unable to pay. Regulations promulgated by the Department of Health, Education and Welfare in July 1972 established numerical guidelines for what the Hill-Burton Act refers to as a "reasonable volume of services." While these guidelines do not require that any particular person who is unable to pay be admitted, they do require that at least some amount of services be provided to this group by every hospital that has received Hill-Burton funds. In addition, the Act authorizes federal assistance for construction of public and nonprofit hospitals and public health centers in conjunction with state-approved construction programs, if state and local resources help to build and maintain the new facilities.

The provisions of the Act and its corresponding regulations have been interpreted by the courts to require a policy of nondiscrimination in administration and use of the facilities constructed, renovated, or maintained under authorized state-approved construction programs. Thus hospitals receiving Hill-Burton funds are subject to the Fifth and Fourteenth Amendments.

In *Simkins v. Moses H. Cone Memorial Hospital,* [323 F. 2d 959 (4th Cir. 1963)], a federal court held that two hospitals were prohibited from denying appointments to physicians on the basis of race. The court also prohibited the hospitals from refusing to admit patients or segregating patients on the basis of race.

In *Smith v. Hampton Training School for Nurses,* [360 F. 2d 577 (4th Cir. 1966)], a federal court reviewed a case involving the dismissal of Negro nurses for eating in the all-white cafeteria of a hospital receiving federal assistance under the Hill-Burton Act. The court relied heavily on the *Simkins* case in deciding that the dismissal constituted unlawful discrimination on the part of the hospital.

The *Smith* case clearly illustrates that the prohibition against discrimination in employment is not satisfied by merely hiring members of a minority group. Once a member of a minority group has been hired, the employer has a continuing duty to treat that person fairly and on an equal basis with all other employees. In the *Smith* case, this duty was clearly neglected when Negro nurses were not allowed to eat in the cafeteria where other nurses ate.

Section 3
HOSPITAL ADMISSION

Although nurses are not directly concerned with the legal aspects of the admission of hospital patients, there are certain situations in which nurses have been found liable for discrimination in admission practices.

Usually no legal problems arise when a hospital accepts a person through formal arrangements made beforehand by the person's physician. On the other hand, there may be legal difficulties when an individual presents himself to the emergency service of the hospital or when a physician with admitting privileges asks that one of his patients be admitted and the hospital does not want to treat the patient.

The courts have been reluctant to depart from the traditional view that no person has a positive right to be admitted to a hospital. Generally, this has been so with respect to charitable and governmental as well as proprietary hospitals. Discrimination in admission practices on the basis of race, color, creed, sex, or national origin may constitute a violation of laws forbidding discrimination. Yet such provisions merely forbid the use of these criteria; they do not establish a positive right to be admitted. In judicial decisions the courts have displayed a marked tendency to adhere to the traditional view but find other bases for imposing a duty upon hospitals to admit persons for care under various circumstances.

Governmental Hospitals

Whether a person is entitled to admission to a particular governmental hospital depends on the statute establishing that hospital. Governmental hospitals are, by definition, the creatures of some unit of government, and their primary concern is service to the population within the jurisdiction of that unit. In all cases a connection with the unit operating the hospital is necessary to entitle one to use the hospital facilities. Some of the statutes cover all inhabitants of the geographic area and, in addition, are broad enough to apply to any person within the area who falls ill or suffers traumatic injury and requires hospital care. However, many of the statutes purport to limit the use of the hospital facilities to residents of the governmental unit operating the hospital.

The statutes which create governmental hospitals sometimes describe the facilities as existing for the benefit of the indigent sick residents in the area. Indigency usually refers to the inability of a patient, or the persons legally responsible for the patient's support, to pay for hospital care. Admission procedures thus encompass the determination of the patient's financial status. This may vary from an affidavit, or a certification by the patient or physician, to a general investigation by an agency of the hospital or a separate social welfare agency.

Not all governmental hospitals are limited to indigent patients. Many are specifically authorized to admit both paying and nonpaying patients. Assuming that a patient meets the legal requirements for admission, he must also show that his physical condition warrants hospital care. Governmental hospitals that are operated as general hospitals may limit their facilities in the same way that charitable and proprietary hospitals do, excluding certain persons on the basis of the ailment or the care required. Contagious diseases, such as tuberculosis and certain venereal diseases, are commonly excluded because it has been found more efficient to treat them in special hospitals or special units. The admission of mental patients is usually restricted to hospitals with special facilities for such patients. Where there is a clear need for immediate hospital care to preserve life or to prevent permanent injury, some statutes provide that the hospital need not comply with specified preadmission procedural requirements, such as proof of indigency, before admitting the patient. Once a governmental hospital has rendered assistance to a person seeking emergency treatment, it must continue treatment in accordance with the applicable standard of care.

While persons who are not within the statutory classes have no right of admission, hospitals and their employees owe a duty to extend reasonable care to those who present themselves for assistance and are in need of immediate attention. With respect to such persons, governmental hospitals are subject to the same rules that apply to nongovernmental hospitals.

NONGOVERNMENTAL HOSPITALS

At common law an individual has no right to aid from another individual or from a hospital. Thus the law imposes no affirmative duty on an uninvolved stranger to go to the aid of another person, even one in obvious distress. In *Le Jeune Road Hospital, Inc. v. Watson,* [171 So. 2d 202 (Fla. 1965)], the *Florida* Supreme Court recognized the following common law principle: "Harsh as this rule may sound, it is permissible for a private hospital to reject for whatever reason, or no reason at all, any applicant for medical and hospital services. . . ."

However, once control over the person is exercised, merely saying that there was no duty to act does not relieve an individual or a hospital of liability if the person is harmed as the result of unreasonable conduct. The exercise of control subjects a hospital and its employees to a duty which can be discharged only by acting in accordance with the appropriate standard of care. Most of the litigation defining when the duty to act arises has revolved around charitable hospitals, but there have been no decisions to suggest that private, for-profit hospitals will be judged according to a different standard.

Also, if an individual's conduct, although not negligent, is responsible for an injury, then a duty exists either to make a reasonable effort to render assistance or to desist from aggravating the original injury. If the original injury is aggravated, liability will be imposed only for the aggravation, rather than for both the original injury and its aggravation.

RESPONSIBILITY TO EMERGENCY PATIENTS

The original Hill-Burton legislation required that each state submit a plan which would provide adequate hospitals and other facilities for all persons residing within its boundaries. The 1970 amendments to the Act place a special emphasis on emergency service. Each hospital's emergency department would be considered in the development of the state plan for providing emergency care for its citizens. Consequently, state legislation imposing upon hospitals a duty to provide emergency care is on the increase. These statutes implicitly, and sometimes explicitly, require that hospitals provide some degree of emergency service. However, the courts have not established a clear mandate that hospitals must admit all patients seeking emergency care.

For example, in *Hill v. Ohio County*, [468 S.W. 2d 306 (Ky. 1971)], a pregnant woman approached a nurse working at her desk in the Ohio County Hospital in *Kentucky* and stated that she was afraid she would not be able to get back to her physician in Illinois before she delivered her baby. Two of the four members of the hospital's medical staff were called to authorize admission, but both refused to do so. That night, after she left the hospital, her baby was born at home (unattended). An ambulance rushed her to Owensboro Hospital about 25 miles from the defendant hospital, but she was dead on arrival. The Court held:

> In the instant case, the decendent was not admitted to the hospital nor was the element of critical emergency apparent. The hospital nurse acted in accordance with valid rules for admission to the facility. The uncontradicted facts demonstrate that no breach of duty by the hospital occurred.

Therefore, the hospital and the nurse were entitled to dismissal the suit as a matter of law.

The rationale of the *Delaware* Supreme Court's decision in *Wilmington General Hospital v. Manlove*, [54 Del. 15, 174 A. 2d 135 (1961)], was based upon a finding of an invitation to the patient to seek emergency care

care from the hospital. The case concerned the refusal of a nurse on emergency duty in Wilmington General Hospital, a charitable hospital, to examine or treat an infant who had been suffering from diarrhea and a high temperature. The nurse tried but failed to reach the child's physician, then instructed the parents to bring the child back the next day when the pediatric clinic was open. The child died several hours later. The court held that where a private hospital maintains an emergency unit, refusal to render service to a person in an "unmistakable emergency" may give rise to liability when such refusal causes injury. What constitutes an unmistakable emergency is itself a difficult question.

The distinction between the *Wilmington General Hospital* case and similar cases is the judicial recognition that a hospital, even a charitable hospital, which maintains an emergency service may not refuse to give treatment without any valid reason to one who appears to, and in fact does, require emergency attention. The underlying theory of this position is that during the time when a person is making a fruitless attempt to obtain aid at the hospital, his condition may be deteriorating. Thus the court is applying the principle that the hospital's operation of an emergency service constitutes an invitation to those in need of aid.

In *Stanturf v. Sipes,* [447 S.W. 2d 558 (Mo. 1969)], the *Missouri* Supreme Court reversed a judgment in favor of the defendant, a hospital administrator who had refused to allow a patient to be admitted because of inability to pay a $25 admission charge. The patient had suffered frostbite of both feet. The court held that the evidence would have sustained findings that the hospital "was the only hospital in the immediate area, it maintained an emergency service, and . . . plaintiff applied for emergency treatment and was refused . . ."

> The members of the public . . . had reason to rely on the [hospital], and in this case it could be found that plaintiff's condition was caused to be worsened by the delay resulting from the futile efforts to obtain treatment from the . . . [h]ospital.

In *Thomas v. Corso,* [265 Md. 84, 288 A. 2d 379 (1972)], the Maryland court sustained a verdict against the hospital and a physician. The patient was brought to the hospital emergency room after being struck by a car. However, he was not personally attended by a physician although he was in shock, as indicated by dangerously low blood pressure. There was some telephone contact between the nurse in the emergency department and the physician, who was providing on-call coverage, but the physician did not come to the hospital until the patient was close to death.

The court reasoned that expert testimony was not even necessary to establish what common sense made evident: that a patient who had been struck by a car may have suffered internal injuries and should have been evaluated and treated by a physician. Lack of attention in such cases is not reasonable care by any standard. The concurrent negligence of the nurse, who failed to contact the on-call physician after the patient's condition had worsened, did not relieve the physician of liability for his failure to come to the emergency department at once., Rather, under the doctrine of *respondeat superior* the nurse's negligence was a basis for holding the hospital liable as well.

The doctrine of *respondeat superior* imposes liability upon the hospital for the legal wrongs of its employees which occur during the furtherance of the employer's enterprise. Imposing liability in this way is justified because the burden of recompensing the person injured is more easily borne by the employer and also because in theory the employer's liability is motivation to supervise employees closely.

Another automobile accident emergency case, *Citizens Hospital Association v. Schoulin,* [48 Ala. 101, 262 So. 2d 303 (1972)], reached a conclusion similar to that of the *Thomas* case. This accident victim sued the hospital and the attending physician for their negligence in failing to discover and properly treat his injuries. The court held the hospital liable because its employee failed to communicate properly to the on-call physician and failed to discover, within a reasonable time after admission, that the patient had a broken back.

LEGAL REPORTING
OBLIGATIONS

A SOCIETY WISHES THE BEST POSSIBLE ENVIRONMENT FOR ITS MEMBERS. IT WORKS through government to protect its people by health regulations and statutes. Only through reliable observations and reports can proper measures be instituted to safeguard the environment of the society. Therefore, the role of the nurse or any other medical professional is very important. Because the medical professional is in a position to observe and gather information about diseases, parental neglect, mistreatment of individuals, and criminal acts, it is every professional's obligation to relay this information to the appropriate authority so that corrective measures can be taken.

Of prime importance to the nurse are health statutes requiring that certain information be transmitted to governmental officials. Although most statutory reporting requirements do not contain an express immunity from suit for unauthorized disclosure, as a general rule the person making the report under statutory command will be protected by the doctrine of privilege. The reporting statutes are the legal means by which the states regulate the health, welfare, and safety of their citizens through the exercise of the state's general police power.

Section 1

ABUSED CHILDREN

The physically abused or neglected child is a medical, social, and legal problem. What constitutes an abused child is difficult to determine because it is often impossible to ascertain whether a child was injured intentionally or accidentally. Even the legal definition of a child varies. In one state a 12-year-old is an adult in the eyes of the law; in another state an 18-year-old is legally still a child. To compound the confusion, some state laws apply to minors but do not specify what a minor is, and others use the word "child" without further definition.

There was a time when health practitioners had good reason to avoid reporting their suspicions about injured children. Anyone who made a report of child abuse to the proper authorities could have been sued by the child's parents on the basis that the report was a defamation of the parents' character or an invasion of their privacy. Health practitioners could also have been liable for money damages if their suspicions were proved wrong.

Today, however, all states and the *District of Columbia* have enacted laws to protect abused children. Furthermore, almost all states protect the persons required to report cases of child abuse. [☞ For a summary of child abuse laws, see Appendix D.]

The various laws differ in their definition of an abused child. Generally, an abused child is one who has had serious physical injury inflicted by other than accidental means. The injuries may have been inflicted by a parent or any other person responsible for the child's care. Some states extend the definition to include a child suffering from starvation. Other states include moral neglect in the definition of abuse. For example, *Arizona* mentions immoral associations; *Idaho* includes endangering the child's morals; and *Mississippi* describes being found in a disreputable place or associating with vagrant, vicious, or immoral persons. Sexual abuse is also enumerated as an element of neglect in the statutes of a few states.

Most state laws require certain people to report suspected cases of abuse. In a few states, although not required to report instances of child abuse, certain identified individuals who do so are protected. The child abuse laws may or may not provide penalties for failure to report. The classification of individuals covered by the various statutes ranges from physicians to "any person". Many of the statutes specifically include nurses.

Any report of child abuse must be made with a good faith belief that the facts reported are true. What "good faith" means is ultimately up to a court when deciding a law suit involving child abuse statutes. But when a health practitioner's medical evaluation is that there is reasonable cause to believe a child's injuries were not accidental, making the report will not result in liability.

All abused child statutes provide protection from civil suit for anyone making or participating in a good faith report. Most states also provide immunity from criminal liability. Even in states that do not, it is extremely unlikely that anyone making a good faith report of suspected child abuse would be subject to criminal liability.

Reporting laws specify the nature and content of the report of child abuse. Almost all the statutes require that when a person covered by statute is attending a child as a staff member of a hospital or similar institution, and child abuse is suspected, the staff member must notify the person in charge of the institution, who in turn makes the necessary report.

Typical statutes provide that an oral report be made immediately, followed as soon as possible by a written report. Most states require that the report contain the following information: the name and address of the child, the persons responsible for the child's care, the child's age, the nature and extent of the child's injuries (including any evidence of previous injuries), and any other information that might be helpful in establishing the cause of the injuries and the identity of the perpetrator.

Section 2
DISEASES IN NEWBORNS

Many states require anyone in attendance at birth to report, either to the physician in charge or to an appropriate health officer, all instances of diarrhea, staphylococcal disease, or other infections. Most states provide for penalizing any violator of these laws.

In particular, health personnel must report inflammation, swelling, redness, or unnatural discharge from an infant's eyes. The *Rhode Island* statute is typical:

§23-13-5 REPORTS OF OPHTHALMIA NEONATORUM
It shall be the duty of any phsycian, midwife, nurse, parent or other person or persons assisting any woman in childbirth or assisting in the care of any infant to report within twelve (12) hours after noting the same, any such case of ophthalmia neonatorum coming to his or her attention, to the department of health.

Statutory reporting requirements are made under each state's police power. States require treatment of ophthalmia neonatorum because public funds might have to be used to train or care for blind children, as well as because the state is interested in maintaining its citizens's health.

Section 3
PHENYLKETONURIA IN NEWBORNS

Phenylketonuria (PKU) is one of the most recent additions to the list of reportable conditions. Actually, the chief concern is to encourage the testing and treatment of infants for PKU. However, some statutes, such as *Nevada's,* still require a report to an appropriate health agency if tests reveal PKU in an infant:

Ch. 442.115 EXAMINATION, TESTING OF INFANTS FOR DISCOVERY OF PHENYLKETONURIA

1. Any physician, surgeon, obstetrician, midwife, nurse, maternity home or hospital of any nature attendant on or

assisting in any way whatever any infant, or the mother of any infant, at childbirth shall make or cause to be made an examination of such infant, including a standard test, to the extent necessary for the discovery of phenylketonuria.

2. If the examination and test reveal the existence of such a condition in an infant, the physician, surgeon, obstetrician, midwife, nurse, maternity home or hospital attendant on or assisting at the birth of such infant shall immediately:

(a) Report such condition to the local health officer of the county or city within which the infant or the mother of the infant resides, and the local health officer of the county or city in which the child is born; and

(b) Discuss the condition with the parent, parents or other persons responsible for the care of the infant and inform such person or persons of the treatment necessary for the cure of the condition.

3. An infant shall be exempt from examination if either parent files with the person or institution responsible for making such examination a written statement objecting to the examination.

Many statutes say that only parents may object to testing for PKU, and only on religious grounds.

The PKU statutes, as well as the statutes related to ophthalmia neonatorum, illustrate the state's power to regulate preventive as well as corrective medicine.

Section 4

COMMUNICABLE DISEASES

Many states have enacted laws which require that actual or suspected cases of communicable disease be reported to the proper authorities. Although other persons are affected, the responsibility for reporting generally falls upon the public health nurse. For example, a *New York* regulation provides:

SANITARY CODE, Ch. 2, REG. 3 (1954). Reporting by others than physicians of cases of diseases presumably communicable.

When no physician is in attendance it shall be the duty of the head of a private household or the person in charge of any institution, school, motel, boarding house, camp or vessel or any public health nurse or any other person having actual knowledge of an individual affected with any disease presumably communicable, to report immediately the name and address of such person to the local health officer. Until official action on such case has been taken, strict isolation shall be maintained.

Statutes requiring the reporting of communicable diseases emphasize the need for such statutes. If the state is to protect its citizens' health through its power to quarantine, the state must have developed procedures insuring the prompt reporting of infection or disease.

Section 5

BIRTHS OUT OF WEDLOCK

The responsibility for reporting births out of wedlock falls primarily upon someone other than the nurse. However, there are situations where a nurse may be the appropriate person to make the report. For example, *North Dakota* provides:

§50-20-03 RESPONSIBILITY FOR REPORTING

Births out of wedlock or with congential deformities which occur in a licensed maternity home or hospital shall be reported by the licensee of such home or hospital. All such births occurring outside of maternity homes or hospitals shall be reported by the legally qualified physician in attendance, or in the event of absence of a physician, by the registered nurse or other attendant.

A state needs a statute requiring the reporting of births so as to keep its records of births and deaths accurate.

Section 6

GUNSHOT WOUNDS

Gunshot wound laws require reports where injuries are inflicted by lethal weapons or, in some cases, by unlawful acts. Some statutes even include automobile accidents within their definition of lethal weapons. The *New York* statute is typical:

§265.25 CERTAIN WOUNDS TO BE REPORTED (Penal Law)
Every case of a bullet wound, gunshot wound, powder burn or any other injury arising from or caused by the discharge of a gun or firearm, and every case of a wound which is likely to or may result in death and is actually or apparently inflicted by a knife, icepick or other sharp or pointed instrument, shall be reported at once to the police authorities of the city, town or village where the person reporting is located by: (a) the physician attending or treating the case; or (b) the manager, superintendent or other

person in charge, whenever such case is treated in a hospital, sanitarium or other institution. . . .

The connection of guns with crime makes this law a valid exercise of police power. Information of this type is also useful for making statistical reports on crime.

Section 7
CRIMINAL ACTS

Besides the subjects specified by statute as reportable, the nurse may have a moral or legal duty to report to the police such acts as attempted suicide, assault, rape, or the unlawful dispensing or taking of narcotic drugs. Much of this information may be learned while caring for patients and would ordinarily be privileged communication. Therefore, care must be taken that only the police are given such information.

GOOD SAMARITAN LAWS

MOST STATES HAVE ENACTED GOOD SAMARITAN LAWS WHICH RELIEVE PHYSI-cians, nurses, and in some instances laymen from liability in certain emergency situations. Good samaritan legislation encourages health professionals to render assistance at the scene of emergencies. By offering immunity, the laws attempt to overcome the widespread notion that physicians, nurses, and others who render assistance in an emergency are likely to be held liable for negligence.

Section 1

PURPOSE

State legislatures have enacted good samaritan statutes for a variety of legal, ethical, and moral reasons. It is a generally accepted legal principle that there is no *legal* duty to assist a stranger in a time of distress. However, if one person caused distress to another, there is a legal duty to assist. This principle extends to physicians, who are not legally bound to answer the call of strangers who are dying and might be saved. However, in our society it is a generally recognized *moral* duty to help a person in distress. Thus physicians have a moral and ethical duty to respond to requests for assistance in medical emergencies. The statement of medical ethics of the American Medical Association includes a provision that recognizes this duty.

Whatever the limits on legal duty, the law does require that anyone who volunteers to aid another in distress assumes a legal responsibility to exercise reasonable care and skill in rendering such aid. Thus the fact that a good samaritan acts in good faith and for no payment is immaterial. It is the act of giving aid that creates a duty and subjects the good samaritan to liability if there is a lack of due care. However, one who is confronted with a medical emergency is not held to the same standard of care as normally is applied in a nonemergency situation.

The first good samaritan law was passed in 1959 in *California* to encourage on-the-spot emergency care and treatment by persons with the proper knowledge and skill. Since 1959, 48 states and the *District of Columbia* have enacted good samaritan statutes. The statutes vary markedly with regard to the persons protected, the standard of care required, and the circumstances provided protection.

Section 2

CONTENTS

PERSONS IMMUNE FROM CIVIL LIABILITY

Of the 49 jurisdictions which have enacted good samaritan statutes, 22 restrict immunity to licensed physicians and registered nurses, and 4 others grant immunity to physicians only. Of the states that grant immunity to physicians, 18 also extend immunity to physicians licensed in any state; 15 states that extend immunity to nurses include nurses licensed in any state. In 23 states, *any* person who renders aid or treatment at the scene of an emergency falls within the coverage of the statute. [☞ For an analysis of good samaritan statutes, see Appendix E.]

SCOPE OF IMMUNITY

Each good samaritan statute provides a standard of care that delineates the scope of immunity for those persons eligible under the law. The standards vary widely from state to state and are often ambiguous. In most states, the scope of immunity is generally qualified by the statement that the person giving aid must act in good faith. Some statutes require that the physician or the person rendering the care must act with "due care," without "gross negligence," or without "willful or wanton" misconduct.

No cases have been found which interpret the language of these statutes or which have imposed liability on a physician or nurse for negligence in rendering assistance at the scene of an emergency. Likewise, there are no cases holding a physician or nurse blameless in rendering care at an emergency.

Despite problems of interpretation, it is clear that the purpose of the statutes is to encourage volunteer medical assistance in emergency situations. The language which grants immunity also supports the conclusion that the doctor, nurse, or layman who is covered by the act will be protected from liability for ordinary negligence in rendering assistance in an emergency.

Section 3

CIRCUMSTANCES COVERED

Under most statutes, immunity is granted only in an emergency or for rendering emergency care. The concept of emergency usually refers to a combination of unforeseen circumstances requiring spontaneous action to avoid impending danger. Some states have tried to be more precise as to what constitutes an emergency or accident. According to the *Alaska* statute, the emergency circumstances must suggest that the giving of aid is the only alternative to death or serious bodily injury. The *Pennsylvania* statute says an emergency is an unexpected occurrence involving injury or illness in public or private places.

Some statutes are so broadly worded that they could include emergencies that occur in an institution. However, because the purpose of the legislation is to encourage assistance where none is usually available, the more extreme definitions will probably not apply.

Most statutes require that emergency services be rendered without payment or an expectation of payment. Apparently this provision was inserted to emphasize that the actions of a good samaritan must be voluntary. Even so, the courts have recognized a physician's right to compensation in some emergencies. For example, physicians have the right to compensation for assisting in rescue operations. In order to be legally immune under the good samaritan laws, however, the physician or nurse must render help voluntarily and without expectation of later pay.

Section 4

EFFECT ON NURSES

Nurses are covered in the good samaritan statutes of 45 jurisdictions. Although the legislation is designed to encourage voluntary emergency care, the laws do provide the nurse with a legal choice: to stop at the scene of an emergency, render assistance, and feel some assurance of protection from liability for negligence; or to pass the scene without suffering legal consequences. In any event, if the nurse chooses to stop and render care, the quality of care must be adequate in light of the circumstances of the emergency.

ABORTION

THE LAW REGARDING ABORTION PROCEDURES HAS UNDERGONE SUBSTANTIAL change in recent years. Medically, an abortion may be defined as "the premature expulsion from the uterus of the products of conception—of the embryo, or of a nonviable fetus." [Dorland's Illustrated Medical Dictionary (24th ed. 1965)]

An abortion may further be classified as spontaneous or induced. It may occur as the incidental result of a medical procedure which is not intended to abort an embryo or nonviable fetus.

The term has been defined legally as:

> The expulsion of the foetus at a period of utero-gestation so early that it has not acquired the power of sustaining an independent life. The unlawful destruction, or the bringing forth prematurely, of the human foetus before the natural time of birth, . . . [s]ometimes loosely used for the offense of procuring a premature delivery; but strictly, the early delivering is the abortion; causing or procuring abortion is the full name of the offense. [Black's Law Dictionary (4th rev. ed. 1968)]

The concern here is the deliberately, directly and voluntarily induced abortion, and the focus is therefore on the legal issues involved in such a procedure.

Section 1

THE LEGAL STATUS OF ABORTION

Medical professionals are currently faced with a twofold problem regarding abortions: First, civil liability may be incurred for refusing to allow abortions or for restricting the circumstances under which an abortion may be performed on the premises. Second, criminal liability may be incurred for allowing an abortion procedure when it is prohibited by valid state statutes. Both the civil and criminal liability aspects have been complicated by recent United States Supreme Court decisions on abortion. In part, these decisions have given further strength and enforceability to a woman's right to privacy in the context of matters relating to her own body. However, the Supreme Court also recognized the interest of the states in protecting potential life and attempted to spell out the extent to which the states may regulate and even prohibit abortions.

ANALYSIS OF SUPREME COURT DECISIONS

In *Roe v. Wade,* [410 U.S. 113 (1973)], the U.S. Supreme Court held the *Texas* penal abortion law unconstitutional:

> A state criminal abortion statute . . . that excepts from criminality only a *life-saving* procedure on behalf of the mother, without regard to pregnancy stage and without recognition of the other interests involved, is violate of the Due Process Clause of the Fourteenth Amendment.

The Court then went on to delineate what regulatory measures a state may lawfully enact during the three stages of pregnancy. In the companion decision, *Doe v. Bolton,* [410 U.S. 179 (1973)], wherein the Court considered a constitutional attack on the *Georgia* abortion statute, further restrictions were placed on state regulation of the procedure. The provision of the *Georgia* statute establishing residency requirements for women seeking abortions and the provision requiring that the procedure be performed in a hospital accredited by the Joint Commission on Accreditation of Hospitals were declared constitutionally invalid. In considering legislative provisions establishing medical staff approval as a prerequisite to the abortion procedure, the Court decided:

> Interposition of the hospital abortion committee is unduly restrictive of the patient's rights and needs that . . . have already been medically delineated and substantiated by her personal physician. To ask more serves neither the hospital nor the State.

The Court was unable to find any constitutionally justifiable pertinence in a statutory requirement of advance approval by the abortion committee of the hospital's medical staff. Insofar as statutory consultation requirements are concerned, the Court reasoned that the acquiescence of two copractitioners has no rational connection with a patient's needs and, furthermore, unduly infringes on the physician's right to practice.

Thus, by using a test related to patient needs, the Court in *Doe v. Bolton* struck down four preabortion procedural requirements, commonly imposed by state statutes, having to do with (1) residency, (2) performance of the abortion in an accredited hospital, by the Joint Commission on Accreditation of Hospitals, (3) approval by a committee of the hospital's medical staff, and (4) consultations.

THE FIRST TRIMESTER

During the first stage or trimester of pregnancy, the state is virtually without power to restrict or regulate abortions; the decision to perform an abortion is between the woman and her physician. A state may require only that abortions be performed by a physician licensed pursuant to its laws. However, a woman's right to an abortion is not unqualified since the decision to perform the procedure must be left to the medical judgment of her attending physician. The right that any woman has in the first three months is to seek out a physician willing to perform an abortion and, if such a physician is secured, to have the abortion performed without intervention by the state. The state has no compelling interest at this stage of pregnancy which would permit it to override the woman's right to privacy by means of legislation.

THE SECOND TRIMESTER

In *Roe v. Wade,* the Supreme Court stated:
> For the stage subsequent to approximately the end of the first trimester, the State, in promoting its interest in the health of the mother, may, if it chooses, regulate the abortion procedure in ways that are reasonably related to maternal health.

Thus during approximately the fourth to sixth month of pregnancy the state may regulate the medical conditions under which the procedure is performed. The constitutional test of any legislation concerning abortion during this period would be its relevance to the objective of protecting maternal health.

THE THIRD TRIMESTER

By the time the final stage of pregnancy has been reached, the Supreme Court reasoned that the state had acquired a compelling interest in the product of conception which would override the woman's right to privacy and justify stringent regulation, even to the extent of prohibiting abortions. In the *Roe* case the Court formulated its ruling as to the last trimester in the following words:

> For the stage subsequent to viability, the State in promoting its interest in the potentiality of human life, may, if it chooses, regulate, and even proscribe, abortion except where it is necessary, in appropriate medical judgment for the preservation of the life or health of the mother.

Thus during the final stage of pregnancy a state may prohibit all abortions except those deemed necessary to protect maternal life or health. The state's legislative powers over the performance of abortions increase as the pregnancy progresses toward term.

STATUS OF STATE REGULATION

The effect of the Supreme Court's decisions in 1973 was to invalidate all or part of almost every state abortion statute then in force. The response of state legislatures to these decisions was varied, but it is clear that a number of state laws have been enacted to restrict the performance of abortions as much as possible. Some of these laws may in fact restrict abortions to a greater extent than permitted by Supreme Court decisions.

Among the subjects considered in recent state statutes are the nature of the facilities in which abortions are performed, the consent of the husband of a married patient, the consent of a parent or guardian of a minor patient, the filing of detailed reports by physicians and institutions regarding abortions performed, the determination by medical consultation of the need for abortion to preserve the woman's life in the third trimester, and the medical care to any aborted fetus capable of life.

These statutes also specifically recognize the right of physicians and hospital personnel to refuse to participate in abortions, without discrimination for their refusal, and the right of hospitals to turn away abortion patients. It is noteworthy that the majority of the Court in *Doe v. Bolton* found no constitutional infirmity in the *Georgia* statutory provisions of this type, sometimes referred to as a "conscience clause." The Court stated that "obviously [they] are in the statute in order to afford appropriate protection to the individual and to the denominational hospital."

Section 2

REGULATION OF ABORTION

The *Doe* and *Roe* decisions of the Supreme Court leave open the question of how far medical professionals may proceed in placing restrictions and prerequisites on those seeking abortions. The subject of both decisions is state regulation of the procedure. However, it is possible that certain hospitals may be found to be instrumentalities of the state or to be associated with the state in such a manner as to be deemed engaged in state action. Civil liability may then result from a hospital's refusal to perform an abortion or from its imposition of requirements difficult to meet, if a patient can show that the hospital's action could be characterized as state action and that her rights were thereby abridged. Existing federal and state legal doctrine regarding both state action and the individual's right of access to facilities for treatment may require some hospitals to provide opportunities for abortion. But to what extent this may hold true is not yet altogether clear.

In *Doe v. Bellin Memorial Hospital,* [479 F.2d 756 (1973)], the U.S. Court of Appeals for the Seventh Circuit ruled that a voluntary hospital which received Hill-Burton funds did not surrender "the right it otherwise possessed to determine whether it would accept abortion patients." Neither did the court find receipt of such funds and other aspects of state regulation sufficient to make the hospital's abortion rules state action.

Hospitals owned or operated by governmental bodies may well be required to allow abortions that are not illegal under valid state laws because their activities are regarded as state action. However, this would not mean that physicians or hospital personnel, as individuals, would be required to participate in the abortion procedures.

All hospitals must restrict abortions in conformity with valid state legislation and must meet the reporting, personnel, and other requirements in such laws in order to avoid criminal liability. It would appear that at least nongovernmental hospitals will have considerable discretion in establishing abortion policy and that such policy matters will be the subject of considerable concern.

STERILIZATION AND ARTIFICIAL INSEMINATION

STERILIZATION IS THE TERMINATION OF THE ABILITY TO PRODUCE OFFSPRING. Sometimes, sterilization is the primary and desired result of a surgical operation; sometimes, it is a secondary consequence of an operation to remove a diseased reproductive organ or to cure a particular malfunction of such an organ. Most sterilizations of reproductive organs that are not diseased are effected by vasectomy in men and salpingectomy in women. A vasectomy merely shuts off the flow of a portion of the seminal fluid. Not only is it a success in an overwhelming number of cases, but a reversal operation is sometimes successful. A salpingectomy blocks the passage between the ovary and the uterus, reducing the likelihood that pregnancy will occur through a natural reopening of the passage.

Section 1

EUGENIC STERILIZATION

The term "eugenic sterilization" refers to sterilization of persons within certain classes or categories described in statutes, without the need for consent by, or on behalf of, those subjected to the procedures. Persons classified as insane, mentally deficient, feebleminded, and, in some instances, epileptic are included within the scope of the statutes. Several states have also included certain sexual deviates and persons classified as habitual criminals. Such statutes are ordinarily said to be designed to prevent the transmission of hereditary defects to succeeding generations, but several recent statutes have also recognized the purpose of preventing procreation by individuals who would not be able to care for their offspring.

About half the states have laws authorizing eugenic sterilization. The decision in *Wade v. Bethesda Hospital,* [337 F. Supp. 671 (1971)], strong-

111

ly suggests that in the absence of statutory authority the state cannot order sterilization for eugenic purposes.

Eugenic sterilization statutes provide at the minimum:

1. A grant of authority to public officials supervising state institutions for the mentally ill or prisons and to certain public health officials to conduct sterilizations.

2. A requirement of personal notice to the person subject to sterilization and if that person is unable to comprehend what is involved, notice to the person's legal representative, guardian, or nearest relative.

3. A hearing by the board designated in the particular statute to determine the propriety of the prospective sterilization. At the hearing, evidence may be presented, and the patient must be present or represented by counsel or the nearest relative or guardian.

4. An opportunity to appeal the board's ruling to a court.

The procedural safeguards of notice, hearing, and right to appeal must be present in sterilization statutes in order to fulfill the minimum constitutional requirements of due process.

The image of castration is commonly evoked by the term "sexual sterilization." However, current statutes generally do not authorize castration—in fact, many laws specifically prohibit it—and most eugenic sterilization statutes provide for vasectomy or salpingectomy. This prohibition against castration, along with provisions granting immunity only to persons performing or assisting in a sterilization that conforms to the law, is an added safeguard for persons subject to sterilization.

Civil or criminal liability for assault and battery may be imposed on one who castrates or sterilizes another without following the procedure required by law. However, provision of liability in eugenic sterilization acts for unauthorized sterilizations should not be construed as an indication that state policy is for or against sterilization per se. The fact that a law has in it a liability provision is no guarantee that liability will follow the sterilization of a person outside the group legally subject to eugenic sterilization if that person consents to the procedure.

Section 2
THERAPEUTIC STERILIZATION

If the life or health of a woman may be jeopardized in the event that she becomes pregnant, the danger may be avoided by terminating her ability to conceive or her husband's ability to impregnate. Such an operation is a therapeutic sterilization, one to preserve life or health. It is the medical necessity for sterilization which renders the procedure therapeutic. Sometimes, a diseased reproductive organ has to be removed to preserve the life or health of the individual. The operation results in sterility, although this was not the primary reason for the procedure. Such an operation technically should not be classified as a sterilization, since the sterilization is incidental to the medical purpose.

Necessary medical or surgical treatment which incidentally destroys the patient's power to procreate is not likely to be contrary to public policy in any state. No basis for distinguishing between such a procedure and one that could technically be called a therapeutic sterilization has ever been judicially recognized. Indeed such a distinction would not seem logical since the purpose of each is to preserve health and life. Therefore, there seems to be no likelihood that any state could impose a penalty for the performance of therapeutic sterilizations.

Section 3
STERILIZATION OF CONVENIENCE

An operation resulting in sterilization of the patient is termed a sterilization of convenience or contraceptive sterilization if no therapeutic reason for such an operation exists. Such operations may be considered in terms of both criminal and civil liability.

CRIMINAL LIABILITY

There was a time when arguments were advanced as to the illegality of sterilizations of convenience, primarily because of provisions in eugenic sterilization laws. However, no authorities proscribe such procedures; and, in light of current judicial decisions and legislation, the possibility that a criminal prosecution will result from voluntary, consensual sterilization is illusory.

CIVIL LIABILITY

Although civil liability for performing a sterilization of convenience with appropriate consent appears unlikely, liability may be imposed if the procedure is performed negligently or without the necessary consent. Several states have enacted specific legislation respecting sterilizations of convenience. For example, the *Virginia* statute provides that upon written request of an adult and his or her spouse, and after giving a full explanation of the consequences of such an operation, a licensed physician may perform the sterilization 30 days after the request. This requirement for the consent of the spouse is inapplicable in particular circumstances specified in the statute.

The consent of the person who is to be sterilized or subjected to an operation that may incidentally destroy the reproductive function should be obtained before the operation is performed. Even if an operation is medically necessary, in the absence of consent the performance of a sterilization constitutes a battery, as does any surgical or medical procedure for which consent has not been obtained.

Several distinctive aspects of operations resulting in sterilization should be stressed. Ordinarily, the patient's consent is sufficient authorization for an operation; however, since sterilization affects the procreative function, the patient's spouse has an interest that could be legally recognized. Therefore, when the operation is primarily to accomplish sterilization, it would seem advisable to obtain the spouse's consent. However, when the procedure is medically necessary and sterilization is an incidental result, the patient's consent alone is sufficient.

Where it is predictable that an operation needed to cure a condition will incidentally destroy the ability to proceate, it is imperative that the effect on the reproductive function be made clear to both patient and spouse. Further, when sterilization is to be combined with another procedure, specific reference should be made to the sterilization. A specific consent form that spells out the effect upon the reproductive process is strongly recommended. Its use should lessen the likelihood that either patient or spouse would say, "I didn't know" or "I didn't give consent" and then bring suit for the loss of reproductive ability. Sterilization of convenience on minor patients may raise particular questions as to what person's consent is necessary, and rules regarding minor consent must be carefully observed.

REGULATION OF STERILIZATIONS OF CONVENIENCE

The U.S. Court of Appeals for the First Circuit has ruled, in *Hathaway v. Worcester City Hospital,* [475 F. 2d 701 (1st Cir. 1973)], that a governmental hospital may not impose greater restrictions upon sterilization procedures than upon other procedures that are medically indistinguishable from sterilization with regard to risk to the patient or demand on staff or facilities. The court relied on the Supreme Court decisions in *Roe v. Wade,* [410 U.S. 113 (1973)], and *Doe v. Bolton,* [410 U.S. 179 (1973)], which accorded considerable recognition to the patient's right to privacy in the context of obtaining medical services. The extent to which nongovernmental hospitals may prohibit or substantially limit sterilization procedures is not clear, but it appears likely that such hospitals will be allowed considerable discretion in this matter.

At least one state, *Kansas,* has enacted legislation declaring that hospitals are not required to permit the performance of sterilization procedures and that physicians and hospital personnel may not be required to participate in such procedures or be discriminated against for refusal to participate. Such legislation, which is more frequent with regard to abortion procedures, is often referred to by the term "conscience clause" and was not found objectionable in Supreme Court decisions striking down most state abortion laws.

Section 4

LEGAL STATUS OF ARTIFICIAL INSEMINATION

Artificial insemination is the instrumental injection of seminal fluid into a woman to induce pregnancy. If the semen of the woman's husband is used to impregnate her, the technique is called homologous artificial insemination (A.I.H.), but if the semen comes from a donor other than the husband, the procedure is called heterologous artificial insemination (A.I.D.).

Neither practice is specifically prohibited by statute or common law in any jurisdiction. Furthermore, there appears to be no risk of liability and no danger of criminal prosecution for the medical personnel or hospital, apart from possible liability for negligence in performing the procedure.

A.I.D. raises several problems with which legislation has begun to deal. The first state to pass a comprehensive statute dealing with virtually all the problems is *Oklahoma*. This statute provides guidelines for the physician and hospital to follow and resolves some of the questions arising from A.I.D. that have been litigated. Subsequent to the *Oklahoma* legislation, a few other states have passed laws dealing generally with the same issues.

The absence of answers to a number of questions concerning A.I.D. may have discouraged couples from seeking to utilize the procedure and physicians from performing it. Some of the questions concern the procedure itself; others concern the status of the offspring and the effect of the procedure upon the marital relationship.

Consent

The *Oklahoma* statute resolves the issue of whose consent should be obtained by specifying that husband and wife must consent to the procedure. It is obvious that the wife's consent must be obtained because, without it, the touching involved in the artificial insemination would constitute a battery.

In addition to the wife's consent, it is important to obtain the husband's consent in order to insure against liability accruing if a court were to adopt the view that, without the consent of the husband, A.I.D. was a wrong to the husband's interest for which he could sustain a suit for damages. Because A.I.D. involves the impregnation of the woman with the semen of a person other than her husband, failure to obtain the husband's consent may raise the issue of whether the woman has committed adultery. Several courts have had to deal with this question in divorce proceedings.

The *Oklahoma* statute also deals with establishing proof of consent; it requires that the consent be in writing and that it be executed and acknowledged by the physician performing the procedure and by the local judge who has jurisdiction over the adoption of children, as well as by the husband and wife.

In states without specific statutory requirements, medical personnel should avoid liability by establishing the practice of obtaining the written consent of the couple requesting the A.I.D. procedure.

LEGAL STATUS OF OFFSPRING

The *Oklahoma* statute resolves the questions which have arisen with respect to the legitimacy of a child conceived by means of A.I.D., the duty of support owed an A.I.D. child by the nondonor husband, the effect of A.I.D. birth upon the child's right of intestate succession, and the right to custody of such a child. The law declares that any child born as a result of A.I.D. performed in accordance with the statute's requirements is to be considered in all respects the same as a naturally conceived legitimate child.

Several states have enacted legislation declaring that children conceived by artificial insemination with the consent of the parents are to be considered legitimate and natural children. *California* has declared by statute that the husband of a woman who bears a child as a result of artificial insemination shall be liable for support of the child as though he were the natural father, if he consented in writing to the artificial insemination. This legislation adopts the position taken earlier by the *California* Supreme Court.

CONFIDENTIALITY OF THE PROCEDURE

Another problem that directly concerns medical personnel involved in A.I.D. birth is that of preserving confidentiality. This problem is met in the *Oklahoma* statute, which requires that the original copy of the consent be filed pursuant to the rules for adoption papers and is not to be made a matter of public record.

Section 5

ETHICAL AND MORAL IMPLICATIONS OF ARTIFICIAL INSEMINATION

There are a variety of religious and ethical views as to the propriety of artificial insemination; and various aspects of A.I.D. and, to a lesser extent, A.I.H. have been questioned. However, the present state of the law does not appear to forbid A.I.H. or A.I.D., and a hospital would not be liable for permitting artificial insemination to take place upon its premises, if consent had been obtained from both husband and wife and if any special statutory requirements had been met. Physicians and nurses involved in the procedure would also not be subject to liability if the proper consent had been obtained.

AUTOPSY AND DONATION

Nurses and other medical personnel who are involved in the operation of hospitals often are confronted with a variety of responsibilities concerning the handling of dead bodies. Failure to fulfill these responsibilities may result in liability.

Section 1

LEGAL PRINCIPLES REGARDING DEAD BODIES

Consideration of legal duties in regard to the utilization, handling, and disposition of dead bodies cannot be divorced from the legal questions involved in determining when death occurs. In many legal contexts, such as in deciding rights to the property of the deceased person, the determination of death does not involve the hospital or its personnel. However, where hospital personnel and physicians are to take action inconsistent with maintaining the life of the patient, risks of liability for the hospital and its personnel are necessarily present. New technology, specifically medical advances in methods for artificially sustaining life and transplanting vital organs, requires consideration of processes and criteria for determining when death occurs.

Until recently, the courts had treated the determination of when death occurred as peculiarly within the competence of the medical profession and as based upon the prevailing opinion within the profession regarding the criteria to be applied. The fact that the decision-making process has important implications for society has led to serious consideration of possible benefits to be derived by providing physicians with more specific and objective guidelines. These guidelines provide the physician with a set of publicly accepted processes and criteria to apply in making professional determinations.

Some steps have been taken to develop such guidelines for the medical profession. Safeguards for the patient and the physician with regard to the processes for determining death are evident in the Uniform Anatomical Gift Act. The Act recognizes the need to avoid any conflict of interest on the part of a physician by saying that the determination of the time of death cannot be made by a physician who is a member of a transplant team. A similar provision is contained in the Report of the Ad Hoc Committee of the Harvard Medical School, which in addition establishes the criteria to be used by the physician in determining death. Legislatures in several states have enacted laws setting forth criteria and processes relating to medical activities to be used in determining the moment of legal death and in related matters.

INTERESTS IN DEAD BODIES

The rule now uniformly recognized in the United States is that the person entitled to possession of a body for burial has certain legally protected interests. Interference with these rights can result in liability. Damages awarded in cases where liability is predicated upon interference with the rights of a surviving spouse or near relative in the body of a decedent are based upon emotional and mental suffering that results from such interference. Thus, for damages to be awarded, the conduct of the alleged wrongdoer must be sufficiently disturbing to a person of ordinary sensibilities to cause emotional harm. Cases involving wrongful handling of dead bodies may be classified into four groups: mutilation of a body, unauthorized autopsy, wrongful detention, and miscellaneous wrongs such as unauthorized sale, refusal or neglect to bury, or unauthorized use of publication of photographs taken after death.

In many states, intentionally mutilating a dead body is a punishable crime and is also a basis for civil liability. Obviously, such acts could be said to cause substantial emotional suffering on the part of those who had loved and respected the decedent. Similarly, an unauthorized autopsy may be disturbing to persons who have an aversion to the procedure, although autopsies have become an accepted and necessary aspect of hospital practice. Thus, where an autopsy is performed without statutory authorization and without the consent of the surviving spouse or a relative whose duty it is to dispose of the decedent's remains, liability has been imposed.

Refusal to deliver a dead body to a person who demands custody and is entitled to receive it has also resulted in liability. There do not appear to be any such cases directly involving hospitals, but if a hospital refused to deliver a body until the decedent's bill were paid or if it retained possession of a body after receiving a proper request for delivery, such refusal would constitute sufficient grounds upon which liability for interference with rights to a dead body could be predicated.

Unintentional as well as intentional conduct interfering with rights to a body has resulted in hospital liability. The case of *Lott v. State,* [225 N.Y.S. 2d 434, 32 Misc. 2d 296 (1962)], involved the mistagging of two bodies in a hospital, with the result that the body of a person of the Roman Catholic faith was prepared for Orthodox Jewish burial and a person of the Orthodox Jewish faith was prepared for Roman Catholic burial. This negligent conduct interfered with burial plans and caused mental anguish, for which liability was imposed.

RIGHT OF SUIT FOR IMPROPER ACTION

Although several persons may suffer emotional stress and mental suffering because of indignities in the treatment of the body of the decedent, recovery for wrongful interference with the body and with proper burial of the body has generally been limited to the person who has the right to possession of the body for burial. Some state statutes delineate an order of the duty to bury the decedent. Others set forth an order of persons authorized to give consent to autopsy, from which the order of devolution may be established. In states without either provision, case law must provide the guidelines. Generally, the primary right to custody of a dead body belongs to the surviving spouse. Where there is no spouse the right passes to the children of the decedent, if any, and then to the decedent's parents.

Section 2

AUTOPSY

Autopsies, or post-mortem examinations, are conducted in order to ascertain the cause of a person's death, which in turn may resolve a number of legal issues. An autopsy may reveal whether death was the result of criminal activity, whether the cause of death was one for which payment must be made in accordance with an insurance contract, whether the death is compensable under workmen's compensation and occupational disease acts, or whether death was the result of a specific act or a culmination of several acts. Autopsies are necessary to hospitals, physicians, and medical science because, aside from providing answers to these specific questions, the information gained from autopsies adds to medical knowledge. Autopsies also are a source of information about the medical practice in the hospital. Hospitals have been sued successfully for harm resulting from the performance of unauthorized autopsies, where the hospitals failed to take adequate precautions to prevent such autopsies.

AUTOPSY CONSENT STATUTES

Recognizing both the need for information that can be secured only through the performance of a substantial volume of autopsies and the valid interests of relatives and friends of the decedent, most states have enacted statutes dealing with autopsy consent. Such legislation seems intended to have a twofold effect: first, to protect the rights of the decdent's relatives; second, to guide hospitals and physicians in establishing procedures for consent to autopsy.

Most autopsy consent statutes can be classified in two groups. One group consists of the statutes that establish an order for obtaining consent to autopsy based upon the degree of familial relationship. Provisions of this type furnish the most precise guidelines to the physician and hospital, enabling them to determine without resorting to other statutes or decisions, who the proper person is to contact for autopsy authorization.

The statutes of the second group contain provisions enumerating those persons from whom consent may be obtained but do not provide an order of priority among them. These laws say that consent is to be obtained from any one of the enumerated persons who has assumed custody of the body for burial. In some states with such statutes there are no additional statutes concerning the devolution of the duty to bury and the right to custody. In these states a hospital must rely upon case law to determine whether a person who requests custody of a body for burial is entitled to such custody and is therefore the proper person from whom consent to autopsy should be obtained. Furthermore, the assumption of custody of the body by a person enumerated in the statutes must be clear before consent to autopsy can be relied upon.

In states which have autopsy consent statutes as well as statutes setting forth the order in which the duty of burial and right to custody of the body devolve upon the relatives of the decedent, the two statutes taken together indicate the proper person from whom consent is to be obtained. In states without autopsy consent statutes, other statutes relating to the duty to bury and right to custody of a body for burial or to donation of bodies or body parts may prove helpful in determining which of the decedent's relatives may give effective authorization for autopsy.

AUTHORIZATION BY THE DECEDENT

Approximately one-half of the autopsy consent statutes provide that the deceased may authorize an autopsy upon his remains. Ordinarily such consent must be in writing. While there should be no problem regarding the validity of the decedent's authorization in such states, as a practical matter it may be difficult to obtain consent because it is undesirable to bring the subject to the attention of most hospital patients. Furthermore, there may be legal as well as practical problems in obtaining authorization for an autopsy from a patient before death if the state does not provide by statute for such authorization. If an autopsy is desired, it would probably be simpler and more effective to obtain authorization from the relative or some other person who assumes the legal responsibility for burial, rather than from the patient before death.

Some states have no specific provision for authorization of autopsy by the deceased, but do permit donation of a person's body or parts thereof to hospitals, universities, or other institutions that operate eye or tissue banks, for use in the advancement of medical science, or for transplantation procedures. A court might construe the donation statute as authorizing the decedent to consent to an autopsy because one purpose, among others, for the performance of autopsies is to advance medical science.

In states where there is neither an autopsy consent statute nor a statute permitting donation that may be construed to include autopsy, it is unwise to rely solely upon the authorization of a decedent to perform an autopsy. This is especially true where relatives of the deceased who assume custody of the body for burial object to an autopsy. Although many cases have upheld the wishes of a decedent with respect to the place of interment or the manner of disposition of the remains, whether by burial or cremation, the courts may not afford the same weight to a deceased's wishes concerning autopsy. In such instances, compelling reasons presented by certain kin of the decedent, especially the surviving spouse, may prevail over the wishes of the decedent.

AUTHORIZATION BY PERSONS OTHER THAN THE DECEDENT

Two closely related concepts are concerned in determining who may authorize the performance of an autopsy. One of these has developed in litigation when a corpse has been mutilated and a person has been permitted to bring an action to recover damages. Such cases ordinarily determine an order of priority with respect to the person who may bring an action. The second concept is that of responsibility for burial of the deceased body and is the basis from which the right of an individual to bring an action for mutilation of a dead body arises.

The order of responsibility for burial is ordinarily the same as the order of preference for bringing an action for mutilation, since the latter arises from the former. The person upon whom the duty to bury the deceased is imposed has the right to custody of the body and the right to recover for mutilation of the corpse and is thus the person from whom authority to perform an autopsy should be obtained.

Where custody of the body has been assumed by the first person in the preference order, that person's consent is sufficient to authorize the autopsy and prevent liability for mutilation of the corpse. If consent to the autopsy is refused, performance of the autopsy could lead to liability, even if some other relative of the deceased sought to authorize it.

What if the first person in order of preference is deceased or mentally incompetent, or is unwilling or unable to assume the responsibility for burial of the body, or fails to do so? It is then necessary to determine who has such responsibility—and has the concomitant right to authorize an autopsy. Fortunately, in many states the order of responsibility for burial is set forth in statutes, and the right to authorize an autopsy is given to the person who has assumed custody of the body for burial.

Several statutes that specifically deal with authority for autopsies indicate who can give authorization when the first person in order of priority is unavailable. Such statutes enable the hospital to determine whose consent is sufficient, and the chance of a successful suit by anyone claiming superior rights in the body is practically nonexistent if the statutory provisions are followed.

In the absence of statutes furnishing a preference order with respect to responsibility for burial or for consent, the order usually followed is surviving spouse, children of the deceased, parents, brothers and sisters, grandparents, uncles and aunts, and then cousins.

When consent for an autopsy has been obtained from a relative who assumed custody of the deceased's body, a court would be likely to consider such consent sufficient and not hold a hospital or physician liable for mutilation of the body in the event that a closer relative, who had been unavailable or who would not assume custody for the burial, should bring an action against the hospital after an autopsy was completed. A court may find that a surviving spouse's unwillingness to assume responsibility for burial is sufficient to permit the right to custody of the body to devolve upon a relative who *is* willing to assume such responsibility. But if the spouse is unable to assume the responsibility of burial for financial or similar reasons, the court probably would not recognize the right of the other relative to bring an action for an unauthorized autopsy.

SCOPE AND EXTENT OF CONSENT

Legal issues may arise as a result of performing an autopsy even if consent has been obtained from the person authorized by law to grant such consent. If autopsy procedures go beyond the limits imposed by the consent, or if the consent to the autopsy is obtained by fraud or without the formal requisites, liability may be incurred. It is a fundamental principle that a person who has the right to refuse permission for the performance of an act has, in addition, the right to place limitations or conditions on consent.

It is especially important that the hospital and its personnel adhere to any limitations or conditions placed upon the permission to autopsy because if such limitations are exceeded, the physician or hospital has no defense on the ground of emergency or medical necessity. The principle involved in limiting the scope of an autopsy has been expressed as follows:

> One having the right to refuse to permit an autopsy to be held has the right to place any limitations or restrictions on giving consent thereto, and one who violates such stipulation renders himself liable, as, for example, where he mutilates the body, removes portions contrary to directions, or fails to return severed portions for burial. [72 Am. Jur. 2d *Dead Bodies,* § 32 (1965)].

While consent to autopsy may also encompass authorization for removal of body parts for examination, a separate question may arise concerning disposal of tissues and organs upon completion of the examination. The question is whether the hospital and its personnel may dispose of such material in a routine manner or use it for its own purposes, or whether the hospital must return the tissue and organs to the body before burial. In *Hendriksen v. Roosevelt Hospital*, [297 F. Supp. 1142 (1969)], permission had been granted for a complete autopsy including an examination of the central nervous system by a scalp incision. Yet the court held that liability might be imposed upon the hospital if the plaintiff could show that all the internal organs had been permanently removed from the body. Pursuant to a *New York* statute requiring the authorization of the next of kin, consent was given for dissection; however, the court held that this statute should be narrowly construed and that separate consent would have to be obtained to retain the internal organs of the decedent.

Consent given with the understanding that organs and tissue could be removed and retained for examination would seem to authorize the hospital to dispose of such materials in a suitable manner or to utilize them after the autopsy. However, the *Hendriksen* decision raises doubts on this matter. Where the party giving consent expressly stipulates that parts severed from the body are to be returned to the body for burial, conduct deviating from this provision may result in liability. Also, it would appear that consent to autopsy does not include authorization to mutilate or disfigure the body. Therefore, if autopsy should involve the removal of exterior body parts and if the physical appearance of the body could not be restored without return of such parts, the hospital may be subject to liability for exceeding the scope of the authorization if the removed parts are not returned.

FRAUDULENTLY OBTAINED CONSENT

It is a long-accepted principle that consent obtained through fraud or material misrepresentation is not binding and that the person whose consent is so obtained stands in the same position as if no consent had been given.

This principle can apply to autopsies when facts are misrepresented to the person who has the right to consent in order to induce his consent. If a physician or hospital employee states as fact something known to be untrue in order to gain consent, the autopsy would be unauthorized and liability may follow.

Section 3
DONATION OF BODIES FOR MEDICAL USE

Recent developments in medical science have enabled physicians to take tissue from persons immediately after death and use such tissue for transplantation in order to replace or rehabilitate diseased or damaged organs or other parts of living persons. Progress in this field of medicine has created the problem of obtaining a sufficient supply of body parts to carry out these techniques. Throughout the country there are eye banks, artery banks, and other facilities for the storage and preservation of organs and tissue which can be used for transplantation and for other therapeutic services.

Organs and tissue that are to be stored and preserved for future use must be removed almost immediately after death. Therefore, it is imperative that an agreement or arrangement for obtaining organs and tissue from a body be completed before death or very soon after death in order to enable physicians to remove and store the tissue promptly.

Every state has enacted legislation to facilitate donation of bodies and body parts for medical uses. Virtually all the states have based their enactments on the Uniform Anatomical Gift Act, drafted by the Commissioners on Uniform State Laws, but it should be recognized that in some states there are deviations from this Act or additional laws dealing with donation.

SUMMARY OF THE UNIFORM ANATOMICAL GIFT ACT

Any individual who is of sound mind and 18 years of age or older is permitted to dispose of his own body or body parts by will or other written instrument for medical or dental education, research, advancement of medical or dental science, therapy, or transplantation. Among those eligible to receive such donations are any licensed, accredited, or approved hospital, accredited medical or dental school, surgeon or physician, tissue bank, or any specified individual who needs the donation for therapy or transplantation. The statute provides that when only a part of the body is donated, custody of the remaining parts of the body shall be transferred to the next of kin promptly following removal of the donated part.

In cases of a donation made by a written instrument other than a will, the instrument must be signed by the donor in the presence of two witnesses who, in turn, must sign the instrument in the donor's presence. If the donor cannot sign the instrument, the document may be signed at the donor's direction and in the presence of the donor and the two signing witnesses. Delivery of the document during the donor's lifetime is not necessary to make the donation valid. A donation by will becomes effective immediately upon the death of the testator, without probate, and the gift is valid and effective to the extent that it has been acted upon in good faith, even if the will is not probated or is declared invalid for testamentary purposes.

In the absence of a contrary intent evidenced by the decedent or of actual notice of opposition by a member of the same class or a prior class in the preference order, the decedent's body or body parts may be donated by the following persons in the order specified: surviving spouse, adult child, parent, adult brother or sister, decedent's guardian, or any other person or agency authorized to dispose of the body. A donation by a person other than the decedent may be made by written, telegraphic, recorded telephonic, or other recorded consent.

The statute provides several methods by which a donation may be revoked. If the document has been delivered to a named donee, it may be revoked by a written revocation signed by the donor and delivered to the donee, by an oral revocation witnessed by two persons and communicated to the donee, by a statement to the attending physician during a terminal illness that has been communicated to the donee, or by a card or piece of writing that has been signed and is on the donor's person or in the donor's immediate effects. If the written instrument of donation has not been delivered to the donee, it may be revoked by destruction, cancellation, or mutilation of the instrument. If the donation is made by a will, it may be revoked in the manner provided for revocation or amendment of wills. Any person acting in good faith reliance upon the terms of an instrument of donation will not be subject to civil or criminal liability unless there is actual notice of the revocation of the donation.

The time of death shall be determined by a physician in attendance at the donor's death, or a physician certifying death, who shall not be a member of the team of physicians engaged in the transplantation procedure.

Section 4
UNCLAIMED DEAD BODIES

Persons entitled to possession of a dead body must arrange for release of the body from the hospital, for its transfer to an embalmer or undertaker, and for its final disposal. The recognition by the courts of a quasi-property right in the body of a deceased person imposes a duty on the hospital to make reasonable efforts to give notice to persons entitled to claim the body. When there are no known relatives or friends of the family who can be contacted by the hospital to claim the body, the hospital has a responsibility to dispose of the body in accordance with law.

Unclaimed bodies are generally buried at public expense; and a public official, usually a county official, has the duty to bury or otherwise dispose of such bodies. Most states have statutes providing for the disposal of unclaimed bodies by delivery to institutions for educational and scientific purposes. Thus unclaimed bodies in the custody of public officials, such as coroners or administrators of governmental hospitals, are subject to use for such purposes. Pursuant to these statutes, the public official in charge of the body has a duty to notify the government agency of the presence of the body. The agency then arranges for the transfer of the body in accordance with the statute. If no such agency exists under the statute, the hospital or public official may be authorized to allow a medical school or other institution or person, designated by the statute as an eligible recipient of unclaimed dead bodies, to remove the body for scientific use.

When an unclaimed dead body is in the possession of a charitable or proprietary hospital, the hospital should notify the public official charged by law with disposing of unclaimed bodies. The public official then arranges for the ultimate disposition of the body, either by burial or by transfer to an institution entitled to obtain it for educational and scientific use.

Certain categories of persons are usually excluded from these provisions permitting the distribution of bodies for educational and scientific use. For public health reasons the statutes do not usually permit distribution of the bodies of persons who have died from contagious diseases. Generally, the bodies of travelers and veterans are also not to be used for educational and scientific purposes.

While the majority of these statutes quite explicitly require that relatives be notified and set time limits for holding the body so as to allow relatives an opportunity to claim the body, strict compliance with the statutory provisions is often impossible because of the very nature of problems that arise in handling dead bodies and the required procedures themselves. Noncompliance in such instances would not appear to cause liability. An example of such a provision is the requirement that relatives be notified immediately upon death and that the body be held for 24 hours subject to claim by a relative or friend. The procedure of locating and notifying relatives may consume the greater part of the 24-hour period following death, and if relatives who are willing to claim the body are located, the body should be held for a reasonable time to allow them to arrange custody for burial. It should be recognized that literal compliance may prejudice the interests of relatives of the decedent.

Similarly, when a body remains unclaimed and the hospital has no way of ascertaining that the decedent was a veteran, delivering or disposing of the body for educational or scientific purposes pursuant to the statute would not appear to cause liability should it later be proved that the decedent was a veteran. Failure to adhere to the statute in such instances is not likely to result in liability.

In some instances, a hospital may be or may want to become a recipient of cadaveric material to be used for science or education. This may be true in respect to bodies of persons held by public officials and other hospitals, as well as the unclaimed bodies of persons dying within the recipient institution. In either case, should a hospital want to receive such materials it must comply with the statutory provisions relating to recipients. The hospital may have to register as an eligible recipient or request that unclaimed bodies be delivered to it, and it may have to post a bond to insure proper use and disposal of the body. In addition, the hospital may be required to maintain equipment and facilities for the preservation and storage of cadavers.

INTRODUCTION TO LAW

THIS CHAPTER PROVIDES THE NURSE WITH SOME BASIC INFORMATION ABOUT THE law, the workings of the legal system, and the roles of the branches of government in creating, administering, and enforcing the law.

Section 1

NATURE OF LAW

The essence of most definitions of law is that it is a system of principles and processes by which people who live in a society deal with their disputes and problems, seeking to solve or settle them without resort to force. Law governs the relationships of private individuals and organizations to other private individuals and to the government, which is the paramount authority of the society. Law that deals with the relationships between private parties is termed private law, whereas public law deals with the relationships between private parties and government. The increasing complexity of society and life in the United States has necessitated a broadening of the scope of public law. Regulating private persons and institutions for the purpose of dealing with the many problems within society has become pervasive.

One important segment of public law is criminal law, which prohibits conduct deemed injurious to the public order and provides for punishment of those found to have engaged in such conduct. A crime is the performance of the proscribed act, and the government criminal law enforces against alleged perpetrators of crimes. Public law consists also of countless regulations designed to advance societal objectives by requiring private individuals and organizations to adopt specified courses of action in their activities and undertakings. Much of the public law contains criminal pro-

127

visions that are applicable when individuals and organizations do not abide by the regulations. The thrust of most public law is to attain what are deemed valid public goals.

Private law is concerned with the recognition and enforcement of rights and duties of private individuals and organizations. Legal actions between private parties are of two types, tort and contract. In a tort action one party asserts that wrongful conduct on the part of the other has caused harm, and compensation for harm suffered is sought. In a contract action one party asserts that in failing to fulfill an obligation the other party has breached the contract, and either compensation or performance of the obligation is sought as remedy.

Law serves as a guide to conduct. Most disputes or controversies that are covered by legal principles or rules are resolved without resort to the courts. Thus each side's awareness of the law and of the relative likelihood of success in court affects its willingness to modify its original position and reach a compromise acceptable to both sides.

Section 2
SOURCES OF LAW

Law encompasses principles and rules derived from several sources. The principles and rules of enacted law emanate from legislative bodies and are set in hierarchical order. Law also is generated by the decisions of courts and the decisions and rules of government agencies.

The Constitution of the United States that was adopted at the Constitutional Convention in 1787 and ratified by the states, together with the duly ratified amendments, is highest in the hierarchy of enacted law. Article VI of the Constitution declares: "This Constitution, and the Laws of the United States which shall be made in Pursuance thereof; and all Treaties made, or which shall be made, under the Authority of the United States, shall be the supreme Law of the Land . . . ." The clear import of these words is that the Constitution, federal law, and treaties take precedence over the constitutions and laws of the several states. The position of a court or agency relative to other courts and agencies determines the place assigned to its decision in the hierarchy of decisional law. The decisions of the U.S. Supreme Court are highest in the hierarchy of decisional law; however, because of the parties or the legal questions involved, most legal controversies do not fall within the scope of the Supreme Court's decision-making responsibilities.

In addition to enacted and decisional law, an extensive body of law is issued by administrative agencies created by legislatures. This law takes the form of administrative rules and regulations valid only to the agency which has promulgated them but not in conflict with the federal Constitution and federal legislation. State agency regulations and rules must also conform to federal law and must not conflict with the particular state's constitution and legislation.

Many of the legal principles and rules applied by the courts in the United States are products of the common law developed in England and, subsequently, in the United States. The term "common law" is applied to the body of principles which evolves from court decisions and is continually adapted and expanded. During the colonial period, English common law applied uniformly; however, after the Revolution each state adopted all or part of the existing English common law, then added to it as needed. Thus the common law on specific subjects may differ from state to state. Statutory law has reenacted many legal rules and principles that initially were established by the courts as part of the common law. However, many issues, especially in private law disputes, are still decided according to common law. The rules of common law in a state may be changed by enactment of modifying legislation; they may also be changed by later court decisions which establish new and different common law rules.

With regard to the law applicable to specific controversies, courts for the most part adhere to the concept of *stare decisis,* or following precedent. In other words, by referring to a similar case previously decided and applying the same rules and principles, a court arrives at a comparable ruling in the current case. However, slight factual differences may sometimes provide a basis for recognizing distinctions between precedent and the current case. And sometimes, even when such differences are absent, a court may conclude that a particular common law rule is no longer in accord with the needs of society and may depart from precedent.

It should be understood that all principles of law are subject to change, whether they originate in statutory or common law. Statutory law may be amended, repealed, or expanded by action of the legislature; common law principles may be modified, abrogated, or created by new court decisions. Thus the law affecting nursing, including not only statutory and common law but governmental administrative regulations and decisions of administrative agencies, is not static; it is in a continuing process of growth and modification.

Section 3
GOVERNMENTAL ORGANIZATION AND FUNCTION

The foregoing sections have introduced the legislative and judicial branches of government and touched on their functions in regard to the nature and sources of law. Now the focus is upon the structure of the three branches of government and the manner in which the functions of one branch relate to the functions of the other two. A vital concept in the constitutional framework of the government, both federal and state, is that of the separation of powers. Essentially, this means that no one branch of government is clearly dominant over the other two; however, in the exercise of its functions, each may affect and limit the activities, functions, and powers of the others.

The concept of separation of powers, which may be referred to as a system of checks and balances, is illustrated in the relationships between the branches in regard to legislation. On the federal level, when a bill to create a statute is enacted by Congress and signed by the President it becomes law. If the President should veto the bill, it would take a two-thirds vote of each house of Congress to override the veto. Or the President can prevent a bill from becoming law by not taking any action while Congress is in session. This procedure, known as a pocket veto, can prevent a bill from becoming law temporarily and may prevent it from becoming law at all if later sessions of Congress do not act favorably on it.

A bill that has become law may be declared invalid by the U.S. Supreme Court, an agency of the judicial branch of government, because the Court decides that the law is in violation of the Constitution.

Individuals nominated by the President for appointment to the federal judiciary, including the Supreme Court, must be approved by the U.S. Senate. Thus in the course of time both the executive and legislative branches can affect the composition of the judicial branch of government. In addition, even though a Supreme Court decision may be final with regard to a specific controversy, Congress and the President may generate new constitutionally sound legislation to replace a law that has been declared unconstitutional. The processes for amending the Constitution are complex and often time-consuming, but they too can serve as a method of offsetting or overriding a Supreme Court decision.

Each of the three branches of government has a different primary function. The function of the legislative branch is to enact laws, which may amend or repeal existing legislation or may be essentially new legislation. It is the legislature's responsibility to determine the nature and extent of the need for new laws and for changes in existing laws. By means of a committee system, legislative proposals are assigned or referred for study to committees with special concerns or interests. The committees conduct investigations and hold hearings, at which interested persons may present their views, in order to obtain information to assist the committee members in their consideration of the bills. Some bills eventually reach the full legislative body, where after consideration and debate they may be either approved or rejected. The Congress and all state legislatures are bicameral (consist of two houses) except for *Nebraska*, which has a unicameral legislature. In a bicameral legislature both houses must pass identical versions of a legislative proposal before it can be brought to the chief executive.

The primary function of the executive is to enforce and administer the law. However, the chief executive, either the governor of a state or the President of the United States, has a role in the creation of law through the power to approve or veto a legislative proposal. If the chief executive accepts the bill through the constitutionally established process it becomes a statute, a part of the enacted law. If the chief executive vetoes the bill, it cannot become law unless the legislature overrides the veto; this usually requires the vote of two-thirds of the legislators.

The executive branch of government is organized on a departmental basis. Each department is responsible for a different area of public affairs, and each enforces the law within its area of responsibility. Most federal law pertaining to nurses is administered by the Department of Health, Education and Welfare. Most states also have separate departments for health and welfare matters, and these departments administer and enforce most state law pertaining to nurses. It should be recognized, however, that other departments and agencies of government may also affect nursing. On the federal level, for example, laws relating to wages and hours of employment are enforced by the Department of Labor; these laws and their enforcement may have substantial impact upon nurses.

The function of the judicial branch of government is adjudication—in other words, it resolves disputes in accordance with law. When a patient brings suit against a hospital, seeking compensation for harm allegedly suffered as the result of wrongful conduct by hospital personnel, the suit is decided by the courts.

Many disputes and controversies are resolved without resort to the courts—by arbitration, for example. However, sometimes there is no way to end a controversy without submitting to the adjudicatory process of the courts. A dispute brought before a court is decided in accordance with the applicable law; this application of the law is precisely the essence of the judicial process.

Section 4
ANATOMY OF A TRIAL

In a trial, the judicial procedure is to ascertain facts by hearing evidence, determine which facts are relevant, apply the appropriate principles of law, and pass judgment. The judgment determines the conduct to be followed. The many technical procedures in a lawsuit can be divided into six major steps: commencement; pleading; pretrial; trial; appeal; and execution.

COMMENCEMENT OF THE ACTION

Lawsuits must be brought within a certain time limit that has been prescribed by law in a statute of limitations. For example, in many states, a suit to recover damages for personal injury caused by negligence must be brought within two years after the injury occurs. If a case is not brought within the prescribed time, the action will be forever barred.

The first step in the trial process is to determine what kind of legal action must be instituted. If the controversy has to do with the performance of a contract, the proper action is for breach of contract; whereas if one person alleges to have been injured by the negligent actions of another, the correct action would be in negligence.

The choice of a trial court where the case will be presented depends upon two things: what court has jurisdiction over the subject of controversy and what geographic district includes the area where one of the parties resides or where the action causing the complaint occurred. For example, a person claiming damages for negligent injury could not file suit in a court which is authorized to hear only divorce matters.

The parties to the controversy are the plaintiff and the defendant. The plaintiff is the person who brings the action and makes the complaint; the defendant is the person against whom the suit is brought. Many cases have multiple plaintiffs and defendants. For example, a husband and wife may sue a hospital and several employees, charging that the employees were negligent in doing their jobs. Or the plaintiff may sue a hospital and a person who is not an employee , (a physician, for example, or perhaps the manufacturer of an elevator). These nonemployees are called independent contractors. They may be joined in the suit as parties defendant because the plaintiff alleges that they all contributed to the injury suffered.

When the preliminary items have been taken care of by the attorney, in consultation with the client, the suit will begin. There are two major methods by which a lawsuit may be formally initiated: First, in some courts an action is commenced by filing an order with the court clerk to issue a paper, called a writ or summons, to the sheriff. This summons orders the sheriff to inform the defendants that they must appear before the court on a particular date. Many states and the federal courts use a second method in which suits are commenced by filing and serving the complaint itself.

Upon delivery of the summons or complaint, prompt notice to the defendant's attorney or insurance company is necessary. The defendant's attorney will need to investigate the matter, decide on strategy, identify and talk to witnesses, and prepare a defense. Notice by the defendant to the appropriate insurance company is also important because a malpractice insurance policy generally requires prompt notice of a suit so that the company can make an early investigation of the facts. When notice to the insurer is required, failure to provide it promptly generally bars any right of the insured person under the policy.

PLEADING

Once the action is commenced, each party must present a statement of facts, or pleadings, to the court. The modern system of pleading requires a setting forth of the facts, which serves to notify the other party of the basis for the legal claim. The first pleading filed in an action is the complaint. In some states the complaint may have been filed as a means of commencing the action; if the action did not begin in this way, the plaintiff must file a complaint.

After the complaint is filed, a copy is served on the defendant, who must ordinarily make some reply within 15 or 20 days. If the defendant fails to answer the complaint within the prescribed time, the plaintiff will win the case by default and judgment will be entered against the defendant. However, in certain instances a default judgment will be lifted if the defendant can demonstrate valid reasons for failure to comply.

Upon receiving a copy of the plaintiff's complaint, the defendant also has the right to file preliminary objections before answering the complaint. In the preliminary objections, the defendant cites possible errors that would defeat the plaintiff's case. For example, the defendant may object that the summons or complaint was improperly served, that the action was brought in the wrong county, or that there was something technically incorrect about the complaint. The court may permit the plaintiff to correct the mistakes by filing a new or amended complaint. However, in some instances the defects in the plaintiff's case may be so significant that the case is dismissed.

At this time the defendant may also present a motion to dismiss, alleging that the plaintiff's complaint, even if believed, does not set forth a claim or cause of action recognized by law. If the objection is sustained, the plaintiff's case will be dismissed. The plaintiff does have the right to amend the complaint or appeal the lower court's action to an appellate court. If the court rules against the defendant's preliminary objections and motions, the defendant is then required to file an answer to the plaintiff's complaint.

In some cases, the defendant also has a claim against the plaintiff and would now file a counterclaim. For example, the plaintiff may have sued a hospital for personal injuries and property damage caused by the negligent operation of the hospital's ambulance. The hospital may file a counterclaim on the ground that its driver was careful and that it was the plaintiff who was negligent and is liable to the hospital for damage to the ambulance.

When the defendant has filed an answer, the plaintiff can generally file preliminary objections to that answer. The plaintiff may urge that a counterclaim cannot be asserted in the court in which the case is pending, that the answer is defective in form, that the counterclaim is not legally sufficient, or that the new matter is not legally sufficient. The objections are disposed of by the court and the case moves on.

The pleading may raise questions both of law and of fact. If only questions of law are involved, the judge will decide the case on the pleadings alone. If questions of fact are involved, there must be a trial to determine those facts. When questions of both law and fact are involved, there will be trial before a jury, with the jury determining the facts and the judge deciding the questions of law.

PRETRIAL PROCEDURES

A number of procedural steps that occur before the trial are specifically classified as pretrial proceedings. After the pleadings are completed, many states permit either party to move for a judgment on the pleadings. When this motion is made, the court will examine the entire case and decide whether to enter judgment according to the merits of the case as indicated in the pleadings. In some states the moving party is permitted to introduce sworn statements showing that a claim or defense is false or a sham. This procedure cannot be used when there is substantial dispute concerning the matters presented by the affidavits.

In many states a pretrial conference will be ordered at the judge's initiative or upon the request of one of the parties. The pretrial conference is an informal discussion at which the judge and the attorneys eliminate matters not in dispute, agree on the issues, and settle procedural matters relating to the trial. Although the purpose of the pretrial conference is not to compel the parties to settle the case, it often happens that cases are settled at this point.

In federal courts as well as most state courts, the parties have the right to discovery—in other words, the examination of witnesses before the trial. The usual manner of conducting the discovery is by presenting inter-rogatories or depositions to the opposing parties. Interrogatories are questionnaires that are answered under oath, usually in writing, concerning the facts in the case. When the interrogatories are presented orally by an examiner, the answers under oath are called depositions. Either party may obtain a court order permitting the examination and copying of books and records such as medical records, as well as the inspection of buildings and machines. A court order may also be obtained allowing the physical or mental examination of a party when that condition is important to the case.

In certain instances, it may be desirable to record a witness' testimony outside the court before the time of trial. In such a case one party, after giving proper notice to the opposing party and to the prospective missing witness, may require the witness to appear before someone authorized to administer oaths in order to answer questions and submit to cross-examination. The testimony is recorded stenographically and filed with the court, and it is entered in evidence as the testimony of the missing witness if, when the trial arrives, the witness is in fact unavailable. This procedure may be used when the witness is aged or infirm and may die or be too ill to testify by the time of the trial.

THE TRIAL

At the trial the facts of the case are determined, the principles of law relating to those facts are applied, and a conclusion as to liability is reached. If the case is argued before a judge and jury, it is the jury's function to determine the facts; however, if the case is presented to a judge sitting alone, the judge determines the facts and applies the law.

Evidence given at a trial consists of testimony or answers to questions put to witnesses on direct examination or cross-examination. Evidence may also include real evidence such as equipment, instruments, devices, and other tangible items which have a bearing on the issues or questions in the case. Generally, witnesses are persons who have a direct connection with some part of the case. They may have seen certain events take place or heard one of the parties say something. In highly technical cases, where the ordinary layman is not qualified to appreciate or properly evaluate the significance of the facts, witnesses are called who qualify as experts in their particular fields. The expert witnesses state opinions in answer to hypothetical or theoretical questions asked at the trial.

At the start of the trial, a jury is selected. A number of apparently qualified people will be selected as a panel, and from that panel the jury will be chosen. After the jury is selected and sworn, the attorneys make opening statements. This practice may vary slightly from state to state, but usually the statement indicates what each attorney intends to prove as the trial proceeds.

After the presentation, the attorney for the plaintiff calls the plaintiff's first witness, and direct examination begins. When the direct examination is completed, the opposing attorney may cross-examine the witness in an effort to challenge or disprove the testimony. After cross-examination the plaintiff's attorney may ask the same witness additional questions in an effort to overcome the effect of the cross-examination. When the examination of the plaintiff's first witness has been concluded, each of the plaintiff's other witnesses is questioned in the same way. The plaintiff's attorney also introduces other evidence such as documents and real evidence.

After the plaintiff's entire case has been presented, the defendant may make a motion for a directed verdict on the grounds that the plaintiff has failed to present sufficient facts to prove a case or that the evidence is not a legal basis for a verdict in the plaintiff's favor. If the motion is overruled, the defendant's witnesses are then subjected to direct examination and cross-examination, and the defendant's documentary and real evidence is introduced.

After all the evidence has been presented, either party may ask the judge to rule that the claim has not been proved or a defense has not been established and that the jury be directed to render a verdict to that effect. If these motions are overruled, the attorneys make oral arguments to the jury and then the judge instructs the jury on the appropriate law. This practice varies widely from state to state and even from judge to judge. Some judges marshal the facts, integrate them with the applicable legal principles, and comment on the evidence as well. Other judges merely state the controlling legal principles. Following the reading of instructions, the jury retires to a separate place to deliberate and reach a verdict. When they have done so they report to the judge, who then renders a judgment based on the verdict.

At the time the judgment is rendered, the losing party has an opportunity to move for a new trial. If the new trial is granted, the entire process is repeated; if not, the judgment becomes final, subject to a review of the trial record by the appellate court.

APPEALS

An appellate court reviews a case on the basis of the trial record as well as written briefs and short oral arguments of the attorneys. After argument, the court takes the case under advisement until the judges consider it and agree upon a decision. An opinion is then prepared explaining the reasons for the decision. Appellate court decisions and opinions are a source of continuing legal information for lawyers, who can prepare themselves by referring to earlier cases that are similar to the case they are considering.

When a case is decided by the highest appellate court in the state, a final judgment results and the matter is ended. The instances when one may appeal from the ruling of a state court to the Supreme Court of the United States are rare indeed. There must be a federal question involved, and even then the Supreme Court must decide whether it will hear a case. A federal question is one involving the Constitution of the United States or a statute enacted by Congress, so it is unlikely that a negligence case arising in a state court would be reviewed and decided by the Supreme Court.

EXECUTION OF JUDGMENTS

Generally, in lawsuits naming hospitals, physicians, and nurses as defendants, a party will seek to recover money damages. Other forms of relief are available, such as an order or injunction requiring the defendant to perform or to prevent performance of an act. The jury decides the amount of damages, subject to review by the higher courts.

If, after the trial and the final appeal, the defendant does not comply with the judgment in the suit, the plaintiff may cause the judgment to be executed. If the judgment is an order that the defendant perform or refrain from performing an act, the failure to obey will be regarded as contempt of court and will result in a fine or imprisonment. If the judgment is for the payment of money, the plaintiff may cause the sheriff or other judicial officer to sell as much of the defendant's property as is necessary to pay the plaintiff's judgment and court costs.

Section 5
THE EXPERT WITNESS

In court, the general rule is that witnesses must testify as to facts; their opinions and conclusions are inadmissible. It is the jury's function to receive testimony presented by the witnesses and to draw conclusions in the determination of facts. These functions are the exclusive province of the jury. But the law recognizes that the jury is composed of ordinary men and women and that some of the fact-finding they will be asked to perform will involve subjects beyond their knowledge. When the jury cannot otherwise obtain sufficient facts from which to draw conclusions, an expert witness who has special knowledge, skill, experience or training is called upon to submit an opinion.

Laymen are quite able to render an opinion about a great variety of nonscientific and general subjects, but for technical questions the opinion of an expert is acceptable. For example, no jury of laymen could be expected to know whether an injury to the sciatic nerve would cause permanent or temporary damage. Therefore, a physician with training and experience in neurology would be asked to review the medical information relating to the patient and offer an opinion about the permanence of the damage.

The question of how much and what type of training or experience qualifies one to be an expert is a difficult one. The American Law Institue, an organization of lawyers and judges, suggests the following definition:

> A witness is an expert witness and qualified to give expert testimony if the judge finds that to perceive, know or understand the matter concerning which the witness is to testify requires special knowledge, skill, experience or training, and that the witness has the requisite special knowledge, skill, experience or training.

In practice, when it becomes evident that expert testimony is required, the attorneys for both sides will secure the services of an expert. When testifying, the expert's training, experience, and special qualifications will be explained to the jury. Then the expert will be asked to give an opinion concerning hypothetical questions based on the facts of the case. It is then up to the jury to determine which expert opinion to accept.

A nurse, especially a nurse with supervisory or teaching experience, may be asked to testify in court as an expert. A supervisory nurse may be called to describe the standard of nursing care in the community when another nurse is being sued for negligence. The jury will then have a standard against which to measure the defendant nurse's conduct. If a nurse is accused of injuring a patient by an improper injection, a nursing instructor might be called to tesify about the usual way of giving infections.

When a supervisory or teaching nurse is not available, an experienced registered nurse may be asked to testify as an expert.

After answering questions for the party that called in the expert witness in the first place, the witness may be questioned and challenged by the attorney for the opposing side. The attorney who requested the expert witness' services is expected to object to improper questions by the other attorney. In the event of an objection, the witness stops giving testimony until the judge decides to uphold or deny the objection and directs that the witness answer or the attorney withdraw the question. The witness need not be able to answer every question; an honest "I don't know" often helps convince the jury of the witness' competence.

Whether a witness who is not directly involved in a case has to testify depends upon the rules of the particular state. A witness who fails to appear in court after being subpoenaed may be fined.

It is important to remember that expert witnesses perform a service for the court. They aid the judge and jury by providing information from which realistic conclusions can be drawn and upon which sensible and fair judgments can be made.

Section 6
WILLS

DEFINITION

A will is a legal declaration of a person's intentions upon death. It generally relates to the disposition of property, the guardianship of children, or the administration of an estate. The central idea is that the person who makes a will can express a choice as to the direction which his property and interests will take after death. A will is called a testamentary document because it takes effect after the death of its maker.

Every state has certain specific requirements for the making of a will. If these requirements are not met, a will is considered invalid and is not probated—in other words, validated by a special court. Nurses need to be knowledgeable about wills because they are sometimes asked to act as witnesses.

WRITTEN AND ORAL WILLS

With one exception, all wills must be in writing. The person who makes a will, called the testator, must sign in front of witnesses who are not named as beneficiaries in the will. If the testator is unable to sign, a third person may sign at the direction and in the presence of the testator. Witnesses must be present and must sign the document. The number of witnesses required varies from state to state.

In some states a will that is entirely handwritten by the testator, known as a holographic will, may be valid. But the will must meet all the legal requirements: It must be in the testator's handwriting, it must be dated, and it must bear the testator's signature. Unless a specific law requires otherwise, a holographic will does not have to be witnessed.

The one exception to the requirement that all wills be in writing is the oral or nuncupative will. A nuncupative will is stated orally by the testator in contemplation of death and before a sufficient number of legally competent witnesses, and it must be reduced to writing as soon as possible. Since most states have either eliminated nuncupative wills or limited them to soldiers and sailors, it is advisable to check the law in each state to determine the applicability of this type of will.

Nurses attending a patient who has expressed the intention to make an oral will should write down their recollections as soon as the patient's statement is completed. They should then send the written memoranda, signed and dated, to the hospital administrator so that the patient's family and representatives may be notified. A patient may declare several wills during a last illness. On each occasion, a witnessing nurse and anyone else who attends the patient should complete the same procedures.

SIGNATURES OF WITNESSES

Most states require that a will be attested to and signed by witnesses in order to be valid. Attestation is the act of bearing witness or vouching that all the required formalities have been complied with. The witnesses must have personal knowledge that the will was signed by the testator and that, to the best of their knowledge, the testator was of sound mind and memory at the time of the signing. It is also the witnesses' duty to insure that the testator is acting freely and voluntarily.

Each state specifies the number of witnesses required to sign the will, varying from one to three individuals. When a state does not require that witnesses sign the will, it usually requires that they testify at the time the will is probated that the testator's signature is authentic.

A witness need not read or be familiar with the contents of a will, except in the case of a nuncupative will. But the witness is required to confirm that the testator declared the document to be a last will, that the testator signed the document in the witness' presence, and that all witnesses signed in the presence of each other.

A nurse who is requested to witness a will may refuse gracefully and suggest to the patient that it might be better to have a lawyer present and to ask friends and relatives who are not beneficiaries to be witnesses. However, when a dying patient tries to make an oral will, the nurse may need to participate because such circumstances require that the dying patient's words be recorded. Obviously, a nurse may then be asked to testify when the will is probated.

APPENDICES

APPENDIX A
Explanation of Admission Consent Form

An admission consent form should be signed as part of the admission procedure. The admitting office personnel should specifically inform the patient of the need for the form. Both inpatients and outpatients should be required to sign the admission consent form upon admission for treatment.

The signing of the admission consent form may be dispensed with when

---

CONSENT UPON ADMISSION TO HOSPITAL AND MEDICAL TREATMENT

PATIENT: _____

                                                  A.M.

DATE: _____ TIME: _____ P.M.

1. I, (or _____ for _____)
knowing that I, (or _____) am (is) suffering from a condition requiring hospital care do hereby voluntarily consent to such hospital care encompassing routine diagnostic procedures and medical treatment by Dr. _____ his assistants or his designees as is necessary in his judgment.

2. I am aware that the practice of medicine and surgery is not an exact science and I acknowledge that no guarantees have been made to me as to the result of treatments or examination in the hospital.

3. Check one:

_____ A. I hereby authorize the _____
Hospital to preserve for scientific or teaching purposes or for use in grafts upon living persons, or otherwise dispose of the dismembered tissue, parts or organs resulting from the procedure authorized above.

_____ B. I will be fully responsible for making other disposition arrangements. Removal of that part from the hospital will be accomplished within 5 days after discharge; failure to remove before 5 days have passed will constitute approval of disposition by _____
Hospital under (A).

4. This form has been fully explained to me and I certify that I understand its contents.

_____   _____
          Witness   Signature of Patient

(If patient is unable to consent or is a minor, complete the following):
Patient (is a minor _____ years of age) is unable to consent because
_____
_____

_____   _____
          Witness   Closest relative or legal guardian

---

a pregnant woman, already in labor, presents herself at the hospital for delivery of a child, because arrival at the hospital may be considered a voluntary submission to the medical and hospital routines and procedures usually associated with delivery of a child. Dispensing with the signing of a consent form is suggested in this instance because the patient may be in such pain as to be actually unaware of what she is signing, thus making the signed consent of no greater consequence than her submission to medical attention.

It should be noted that this exception to the general rule requiring an admission consent form does not apply when the patient is not in labor when admitted. Where delivery is to be by means of cesarean section, or labor is to be artificially induced after admission, or the patient requires other special procedures or anesthesia, the admission consent form should be signed when the patient is admitted to the hospital. In some of these situations, a special consent form may be required.

Paragraph 1. The consent form is designed to cover all procedures in the hospital which do not require a special consent form, including routine laboratory, diagnostic, and medical treatment as well as most outpatient care. It provides protection for procedures done by hospital personnel, attending physicians and assistants, or any other physicians called into the case. The form has the merit of providing personal coverage for all persons who have a legitimate reason for touching or ministering to the patient, thus protecting the hospital and the medical staff personnel. Blanks are provided for the name of anyone who consents on behalf of a patient who is physically unable or legally incompetent to consent. A blank is provided for the name of the attending physician. If two or more physicians are attending the patient, all names should be included. The form also provides coverage for the assistants and designees of the physician.

Paragraph 2. The courts have uniformly held that a patient can recover for damages, despite consent, if it can be shown that the physician guaranteed the success of the operation or treatment, and if the procedure was not successful. This paragraph provides evidence that no such guarantee was made.

Paragraph 3. These alternative paragraphs permit the hospital to carry out routine procedures for the disposal of specimens, tissues, and organs taken from the patient and also relieve the hospital of responsibility for their disposal.

Paragraph 4. This paragraph satisfies the requirement that the consent must be given with understanding; it does this by requiring the patient to agree only after proper disclosure that a variety of procedures may be performed.

Signature Block. Lines are provided for signature by the patient or someone authorized to consent for the patient. Space is also provided for the signing of a witness although no witness is required to make the consent effective. Obtaining a witness who can attest to the genuineness of the patient's signature and competency to sign the form is advisable. One witness would suffice to prove the circumstances of the signing. Formalizing the signing of the consent form by having more than one witness may introduce a degree of solemnity that may affect the patient's morale.

APPENDIX B
Explanation of Special Consent Form

The special consent form should not be completed in the admissions office of the hospital. Providing the necessary information and answers to the patient's questions requires knowledge of medicine that only a physician possesses. If a procedure that normally calls for the use of a special consent form is to be performed shortly after admission, the physician may be able to provide the information and procure the patient's consent in the physician's office.

Use of the special consent form presupposes a pattern for disclosure in the conversations between the physician and the patient so that necessary matters are covered. Without a disclosure pattern that provides the patient with the necessary information, the form offers few benefits, because it is the full disclosure documented on the form which provides the protection from possible liability.

With some modifications, the special consent form can easily be adapted for surgical diagnostic procedures such as exploratory operations, as well as for nonsurgical diagnostic procedures that require either general anesthesia or the injection of a foreign substance into the blood stream.

A signed special consent form should be procured before any of the following procedures are carried out:

1. Major or minor surgery which involves an entry into the body, either through an incision or one of the natural body openings.

2. All procedures in which anesthesia is used, regardless of whether an entry into the body is involved.

3. Nonsurgical procedures involving more than a slight risk of harm to the patient or the risk of a change in the patient's body structure. These procedures would include diagnostic procedures such as myelograms, arteriograms, and pyelograms.

4. Procedures involving the use of cobalt and X-ray therapy.

5. Electroshock therapy.

6. Experimental procedures.

7. All other procedures which require a specific explanation to the patient as determined by the medical staff. Any doubts as to the necessity of attaining a special consent from the patient should be resolved in favor of procuring the consent.

The special consent form should be completed at the time the physician explains to the patient the diagnostic or therapeutic procedure to be performed.

Time of the consent. The exact time that consent is procured is important because it may provide evidence that the patient was competent to sign and was not under preoperative sedation. The time is particularly important if the form is signed on the same day that the procedure is carried out; otherwise, it may be inferred that the patient signed the form while incompetent.

147

Paragraph 1. A space is provided so that the condition that is to be treated can be explained and the need for treatment stated. The reason for

---

SPECIAL CONSENT TO OPERATION
OR OTHER PROCEDURE

Patient: _____   Date: _____

Time: _____a.m.
                     p.m.

1.   I hereby authorize Dr. _____ and/or such assistants as may be selected by him, to remedy the condition or conditions which appear indicated by the diagnostic studies already performed.

_____
(Explain the nature of the condition and the need to remedy such condition)

2.   The procedure(s) necessary to remedy my condition (has, have) been explained to me by Dr. _____ and I understand the nature of the procedure to be: _____
(A description of the procedure(s) in the language of laymen)

_____

3.   It has been explained to me that, during the course of the operation, unforeseen conditions may be revealed that necessitate an extension of the original procedure(s) or different procedure(s) than those set forth in Paragraph 2. I therefore authorize and request that the above named surgeon, his assistants, or his designees perform such surgical procedures as are necessary and desirable in the exercise of professional judgment. The authority granted under this Paragraph 3 shall extend to remedying all conditions that require treatment and are not known to Dr. _____ at the time the operation is commenced.

4.   I have been made aware of certain risk(s) and consequences that are associated with the procedure(s) described in Paragraph 2. These are: _____

_____
(A description of the risks and consequences

_____
that are involved in this particular procedure)

_____

5.   I have also been informed there are other risks such as severe loss of blood, infection, cardiac arrest, etc., that are attendant to the performance of any surgical procedure. I am aware that the practice of medicine and surgery is not an exact science and I acknowledge that no guarantees have been made to me concerning the results of the operation or procedure.

6.   I consent to the administration of anesthesia to be applied by or under the direction and supervision of Dr. _____

_____   _____
Witness   Signature of Patient

(If patient is unable to sign or is a minor, complete the following):
Patient (is a minor _____ years of age) and is unable to sign because

_____

_____

_____   _____
Witness   Closest relative or legal guardian

placing the emphasis on the condition is that courts have found it easier to infer that a patient has consented to all reasonable steps to remedy a condition, though the method used may differ from the one explained to the patient. When the form is used for a diagnostic procedure, the nature of the condition disclosed by the tentative diagnosis should be stated in the space provided.

Paragraph 2. Naming the physician who explained the contemplated procedure to the person signing the form reinforces the statement that an explanation took place. Placing the burden of explanation upon the patient's physician is consonant with the physician-patient relationship and guarantees that the procedure will be explained by one competent to do so. The description on the consent form should be written in language understandable to the layman. This manner of explanation will help support the position that the patient received an understandable explanation of the procedure. In the absence of such an understanding, a patient's consent may be deemed ineffective.

If another procedure to treat the same or another condition becomes necessary at some later date during the patient's hospitalization, a second consent form should be procured. If it is known when consent is being initially procured that a series of procedures is indicated over a period of time, then the series can be described and consent to the entire course of treatment procured.

When the form is used for a diagnostic procedure, a description of the procedure should be stated in the space provided. It is also suggested that the physician explain to the patient and note on the form the most likely remedial procedures necessary if the tentative diagnosis is confirmed.

Paragraph 3. This paragraph is inserted to negate the possible contention that the surgeon is limited to the specific procedures described in Paragraph 2, and should provide authority for an extension or modification of the procedure or for the performance of other medically indicated procedures. Explicit consent for additional or different procedures where indicated avoids the danger of complete reliance upon an implication of consent for additional procedures that would otherwise have to be drawn from the consent for a specific procedure.

When the form is used for a diagnostic procedure, the physician should explain to the patient that the diagnostic procedure may reveal the need for remedial surgery at the time, in preference to a second surgical procedure at a later date. If the remedial surgery does not fall within an emergency situation or within the scope of the alternatives in Paragraph 2, then it should not be performed.

Paragraph 4. This explanation must cover the risks and consequences which are associated with each particular procedure described in Paragraph 2. For example, a plastic surgery procedure involving face and neck may carry the associated risk of facial or vocal cord paralysis; a colostomy may result in the patient's bowel movement occurring from an opening in the abdomen. Courts have found consent lacking where a patient was not apprised of risks that are associated with the procedure. Consent has also been found lacking when consequences that ordinarily follow a procedure are not mentioned to the patient.

Paragraph 5. Certain risks are attendant on all surgical procedures, and it is necessary to mention that these risks may materialize without malpractice or lack of due care. If a physician should guarantee the success of an operation or treatment and the operation is unsuccessful, the patient can recover in a lawsuit against the physician even if the physician can show that the patient gave consent. The second sentence of the paragraph provides evidence that no such guarantee was made.

Paragraph 6. If the surgeon selects the anesthetic and provides an explanation to the patient, the name of the surgeon should be inserted in the space provided. Hospitals in which the anesthesiologist is responsible for choosing the anesthetic and providing the explanation to the patient should require that a separate consent form for anesthesia be used and Paragraph 6 lined off.

By adding certain language to the special consent form, a hospital may adapt that form to situations involving experimental procedures or drugs. In certain instances, however, the hospital should draft special forms. For example, the hospital should use a special consent form for requests for inoculation, ritual circumcision, and the taking of photographs.

APPENDIX C
A Sample Nurse's Professional Liability Policy

Declaration of Contents

Insurer	THE X INSURANCE COMPANY 111 MAIN ST., CHICAGO, ILL.
Agent	SMITH & JONES CO., AGENTS 222 SOUTH ST., PITTSBURGH, PENNA.
Insured	MISS IDA GREEN 333 ELM ST., PITTSBURGH, PENNA.
Policy period	FROM JANUARY 1, 1969 TO JANUARY 1, 1970

Liability limits	each claim . . . . $ 40,000 aggregate $120,000
Premium	yearly. $7.00

Pending actions	The named insured represents that no claims, demands, or legal actions are pending against the named insured arising out of any actual or alleged error, mistake, or malpractice.

The insurer named in the declaration of contents contracts with the named insured, named in the declaration of contents, in consideration of the paying of the stated premium and in reliance upon the statements made in the declaration and subject to all of the terms of this policy:

INSURING AGENT
1. Coverage
   A. Malpractice Liability—to pay on behalf of the insured all sums which the insured shall become legally obligated to pay as damages because of injury arising out of malpractice, error, or mistake in rendering or failing to render nursing services.

DEFENSE AND SETTLEMENT
The insurance company under this policy shall:
   A. Defend any suit against the named insured alleging injury to persons and/or property and which is seeking damages that are payable under this policy.
   B. Make any settlement of any claim or suit as it determines expedient.

POLICY PERIOD

This policy is applicable only to accidents occurring during the stated policy period.

CONDITIONS

1. Notice of Occurrence—When the insured knows of any alleged accident covered herein, he shall notify the company as soon as possible.
2. Notice of Claim—When any claim is instituted against the insured, he must immediately notify the company in writing and forward every notice or summons he or his representative has received.
3. Assistance—The insured must assist the company upon the company's request and such assistance shall include attending all hearings and trials and the giving of evidence. The insured must also assist in making settlements upon request of the company.
4. Other Insurance—If the insured has other insurance against a loss included under this policy's coverage, this company will pay its pro rata share of the loss.
5. Assignment—The insured cannot assign any interest in this policy, unless he receives written authorization from a properly authorized representative of the company. Every other attempt to assign the insured's interest shall not be effective.
6. Subrogation—Whenever the company makes any payment under this policy, the company will be subrogated to all of the rights of the insured to recover against any other person.
7. Changes—No agent of the company may change any section of this policy unless he receives written authorization from the company.
8. Cancellation—The insured may cancel this policy at any time by returning the policy to any agent of the company.
9. Limits of Liability—The liability of this policy shall be limited by the declaration applicable to "each claim" on each claim or suit. The liability of this policy shall be limited by the declaration applicable to "aggregate" for the total liability of the company.

_____   _____
Signature of Agent   Signature of Named Insured

_____
Witness

_____
Witness

APPENDIX D

STATE-BY-STATE
SUMMARY OF
CHILD ABUSE LAWS

APPENDIX D

STATE-BY-STATE SUMMARY OF CHILD ABUSE LAWS

State	Citation	Applies to
Alabama	Ala. Code tit. 27, §§21-25 (Supp. 1973).	Hospitals, clinics, sanitariums, doctors, physicians, surgeons, nurses, school teachers, pharmacists, social workers, any other person called upon to render aid or medical assistance.
Alaska	Alaska Stat. §§47.17.010 to 47.17.070 (1971).	1. Practitioner of healing arts, school teachers, social workers, peace officers and officers of the division of corrections, administrative officers of institutions. 2. Any other person.
Arizona	Ariz. Rev. Stat. Ann. §13-842.01 (Supp. Pamphlet 1973).	Physician.
Arkansas	Ark. Stat. Ann. §§42-801 to 42-806 (Supp. 1973).	1. Doctors of medicine, doctors of dentistry, coroners, osteopaths, hospital interns, resident physicians, chiropractors, pharmacists, nurses, laboratory technicians, superintendents or managers of hospitals. 2. Any other person.
California	Cal. Penal Code §11161.5 (West Supp. 1974).	Physician, surgeon, dentist, resident, intern, podiatrist, chiropractor, religious practitioner, registered nurse employed by a public health agency, school superintendent or principal, supervisors of child welfare and attendance, certificated pupil personnel employee, teacher, licensed day care worker, social worker.
Colorado	Colo. Rev. Stat. Ann. §§22-10-1 to 22-107 (Supp. 1969), as amended, (Supp. 1971).	1. Physician, medical institution, nurse, school employee, social worker. 2. Other person.
Connecticut	Conn. Gen. Stat. Rev. §17-38a (1973).	Physician, surgeon, resident, intern, registered nurse, licensed practical nurse, medical examiner, school teacher, principal, social worker, police officer, clergyman.
Delaware	Del. Code Ann. tit. 16 §§1001 to 1008 (Supp. 1972).	1. Physician, any person in healing arts, intern, nurse, school employee, social worker, psychologist, medical examiner. 2. Any other person.
Florida	Fla. Stat. Ann. §828.041 (Supp. 1974).	Physician, dentist, podiatrist, optometrist, intern, resident, nurse, teacher, social worker, employee of a public or private facility serving children.
Georgia	Ga. Code Ann. §§74-109 to 74-11 (1973).	Doctor of medicine, osteopath, intern, resident, dentist, podiatrist, public health nurse, welfare worker, employee of local public school, state recreation personnel
Hawaii	Hawaii Rev. Stat. §§350-1 to 350-5 (1968), as amended, (Supp. 1973).	1. Doctor of medicine, osteopathy, dentistry, or any of the other healing arts, registered nurse, school teacher, social worker, coroner. 2. Any other person.

Age Limit	Report to	Immunity Provision?	Physician-Patient Privilege Applicable?	Penalty?
6	Chief of police, sheriff, Department of Pensions and Security.	yes	yes	MISDEMEANOR. SENTENCE: 6 MO. OR $500.
6	Department of Health and Welfare, peace officer.	yes	yes	
6	Municipal or county peace officer, person in charge of hospital.	yes	yes	MISDEMEANOR. SENTENCE: 10 DAYS, $100, OR BOTH.
6	Person in charge of institution who shall notify appropriate police authority, county and state welfare departments.	yes	yes	MISDEMEANOR. SENTENCE: 6 MO., $500, OR BOTH.
2	Local police authority, juvenile probation department, county welfare department, county health department.	yes		MISDEMEANOR. SENTENCE: 6 MO., $500, OR BOTH (§11162).
Child	Proper law enforcement agency.	yes	yes	
8	Person in charge of hospital, school, or social welfare agency, state commissioner of health, state welfare commissioner, local police department, state police.	yes		
8	Person in charge of institution, Department of Health and Social Services.	yes	yes	SENTENCE: 15 DAYS, $100, OR BOTH.
7	Person in charge of institution, Department of Health and Rehabilitative Services.	yes	yes	MISDEMEANOR OF SECOND DEGREE. SENTENCE: 60 DAYS, $500, OR BOTH.
8	Person in charge of institution, county health officer.	yes		
Minor	Person in charge of medical facility, Department of Social Services and Housing.	yes	yes	

State	Citation	Applies to
Idaho	Idaho Code §§16-1624 to 16-1643 (Supp. 1973).	1. Physicians, resident, intern, nurse, coroner, school teacher, day care personnel, social worker. 2. Any other person.
Illinois	Ill. Ann. Stat. Ch. 23, §§2041 to 2047 (Smith-Hurd 1968), as amended, (Supp. 1974).	Physician, surgeon, dentist, osteopath, chiropractor, podiatrist, Christian Science practitioner, school teacher or administrator, truant officer, social worker or administrator, registered nurse, licensed practical nurse, law enforcement officer.
Indiana	Ind. Ann. Stat. §§12-3- 4.1-1 to 12-3-4.1-6 (1973).	Any person.
Iowa	Iowa Code Ann. §§235A.1 to 235A.8 (1969).	1. Physician, surgeon, osteopath, dentist, optometrist, podiatrist, chiropractor, resident, intern, registered nurse. 2. Any other person.
Kansas	Kan. Stat. Ann. §§38-716 to 38-722 (1973).	Doctor of medicine or dentistry, licensed osteopathic physician, certified psychologist, doctor of chiropractic, resident, intern, social or case worker, registered nurse, school nurse, teacher, school administrator or employee, law enforcement officer.
Kentucky	Ky. Rev. Stat. Ann. §199.335 (1973).	1. Physician, osteopath. 2. Any other person.
Louisiana	La. Rev. Stat. Ann. §14.403 (Supp. 1974).	Any person having responsibility for child.
Maine	Me. Rev. Stat. Ann. tit. 22, §§3851 to 3855 (Supp. 1974).	Doctor of medicine or osteopathy, intern, resident, chiropractor.
Maryland	Md. Ann. Code art. 27, §35A (Supp. 1973).	1. Physician, surgeon, psychologist, dentist, and any other person authorized to engage in practice of healing, resident, intern, registered or practical nurse, educator, mental health or social worker, law enforcement officer. 2. Any other person.
Massachusetts	Mass. Ann. Laws c. 119, §§51a to 51g (Supp. 1973).	Physician, intern, medical examiner, dentist, nurse, public or private school teacher, educational administrator, guidance or family counselor, probation officer, social worker, policeman.
Michigan	Mich. Comp. Laws Ann. §§722.571 to 722.575 (1968), as amended, (Supp. 1974).	Physician, registered nurse, social worker, school principal, assistant principal, counselor, law enforcement officer.
Minnesota	Minn. Stat. Ann. §626.554 (Supp. 1974).	Physician, surgeon, person authorized to engage in practice of healing, hospital superintendent or manager, nurse, pharmacist.
Mississippi	Miss. Code Ann. §§43-21-5, 43-21-11, 43-21-25, 43-21-27 (1973).	Doctor of medicine, dentist, intern, resident, registered nurse.

Age Limit	Report to	Immunity Provision?	Physician-Patient Privilege Applicable?	Penalty?
18	Person in charge of institution, proper law enforcement agency.	yes	yes	
16	Department of Children and Family Services, local law enforcement agency.	yes	yes	
Child	County department of public welfare, law enforcement agency.	yes	yes	MISDEMEANOR.SENTENCE: 30 DAYS, $100, OR BOTH
18	Person in charge of institution, county Department of Social Welfare and county attorney, appropriate law enforcement agency.	yes	yes	
18	Person in charge of institution, county juvenile court, Department of Social Welfare.	yes	yes	MISDEMEANOR.
18	Person in charge of institution, Department of Child Welfare, appropriate police authority.	yes	yes	MISDEMEANOR.SENTENCE: NOT LESS THAN $10 OR MORE THAN $100.
17	Person in charge of institution, police department, Department of Public Safety, Division of State Police.	yes	yes	MISDEMEANOR.SENTENCE: 6 MO., $500, OR BOTH.
16	Person in charge of institution, State Department of Health and Welfare, Division of Child Welfare, county attorney.	yes		MISDEMEANOR.SENTENCE: 6 MO., $100, OR BOTH.
18	Person in charge of institution, local department of social services or law enforcement agency, local state's attorney.	Civil	yes	FELONY. SENTENCE: 15 YEARS.
16	Person in charge of institution, Department of Public Welfare.	yes	yes	
17	Person in charge of institution, prosecuting attorney, probate court, county Department of Social Welfare, State Department of Social Services.	yes	yes	MISDEMEANOR.
Minor	Appropriate police authority, county welfare agency.	yes	yes	MISDEMEANOR.
18	Person in charge of institution, county youth court or family court, county welfare department.	yes	yes	MISDEMEANOR.SENTENCE: 6 MO., $500, OR BOTH.

State	Citation	Applies to
Missouri	Mo. Ann. Stat. §§210.105 to 210.108 (Supp. 1974).	Physician, surgeon, dentist, chiropractor, podiatrist, Christian Science or other health practitioner, registered nurse, school nurse, teacher, social worker or others with responsibility for care of children for financial remuneration, any hospital.
Montana	Mont. Rev. Codes Ann. §§10-1300 to 10-1322 (Supp. 1974).	1. Physician, nurse, teacher, social worker, attorney, law enforcement officer. 2. Any other person.
Nebraska	Neb. Rev. Stat. §28-481 to 28-484 (Cum. Supp. 1972).	Any person.
Nevada	Nev. Rev. Stat. §§200.501 to 200.508 (1973).	Physician, surgeon, dentist, osteopath, chiropractor, optometrist, resident, intern, superintendent or manager of hospital, nurse, attorney, clergyman, social worker, school authority and teacher, licensed child care facility or children's camp employee.
New Hampshire	N.H. Rev. Stat. Ann. §§169:37 to 169:45 (Supp. 1973).	Any person.
New Jersey	N.J. Rev. Stat. §§9:6-8.1 to 9:6-8.20 (Supp. 1974).	1. Doctor of medicine, osteopath, resident, intern. 2. Any other person.
New Mexico	N.M. Stat. Ann. §§13-14-14.1 to 13-14-14.2 (Supp. 1973).	1. Licensed physician, resident, intern, registered or visiting nurse, school teacher, social worker, law enforcement officer. 2. Any other person.
New York	N.Y. Soc. Serv. Law §§411 to 428 (McKinney Supp. 1973).	1. Physician, surgeon medical examiner, coroner, dentist, osteopath, optometrist, chiropractor, podiatrist, resident, intern, registered nurse, Christian Science practitioner, hospital personnel, social services worker, school official, day care center director, peace officer, mental health professional. 2. Any other person.
North Carolina	N.C. Gen. Stat. §§110-115 to 110-122 (Supp. 1973).	Any professional person with reasonable cause to suspect or any other person having knowledge.
North Dakota	N.D. Cent. Code §§50-25-01 to 50-25-05 (Supp. 1973).	Doctor of medicine, osteopathic physician, chiropractor, intern, resident, public health nurse.
Ohio	Ohio Rev. Code Ann. §2151-421 (Page Supp. 1973).	Physician, intern, resident, dentist, podiatrist, practitioner of a limited branch of medicine, registered nurse, visiting nurse, school teacher, school authority, social worker, faith healer.

Age Limit	Report to	Immunity Provision?	Physician-Patient Privilege Applicable?	Penalty?
17	County welfare officer, county juvenile officer.	yes	yes	MISDEMEANOR.
18	Person in charge of institution, county attorney, Department of Social and Rehabilitation Services.	yes	yes	
ild or any competent disabled rson.	County Attorney.			MISDEMEANOR. SENTENCE: $100.
18	Person in charge of institution, police department or sheriff's office, welfare division of Department of Human Resources.	yes	yes	MISDEMEANOR.
18	Person in charge of institution; Bureau of Child and Family Services, Division of Welfare, Department of Health and Welfare.	yes	yes	MISDEMEANOR.
18	Person in charge of institution, county prosecutor, Bureau of Children's Services.	yes		MISDEMEANOR.
18 (3-14-3.A)	County Social Services Office, Probation Services Office.	yes	yes	MISDEMEANOR. SENTENCE: $25 to $100.
16	Person in charge of institution, social services official.	yes	yes	MISDEMEANOR (CLASS A).
16	County director of social services.	yes	yes	
18	Director of Division of Child Welfare of Public Welfare Board, juvenile commissioner, state's attorney.	yes	yes	
18 or any crippled or otherwise physically or mentally handicapped child under 21.	Person in charge of institution, municipal or county peace officer, county Department of Welfare, Children's Services Board.	yes	yes	

State	Citation	Applies to
Oklahoma	Okla. Stat. Ann. tit. 21, §§845 to 848 (Supp. 1974).	1. Physician, surgeon, doctor of medicine, dentist, osteopath, resident, intern, registered nurse. 2. Every other person.
Oregon	Ore. Rev. Stat. §418. 740 to 418. 775 (1973).	Physician, intern, dentist, school teacher, school nurse, public health nurse employed by local health department, employee of public welfare division or a county welfare commission (with permission of his supervisor), police officer.
Pennsylvania	Pa. Stat. Ann. tit. 11, §§2101 to 2110 (Supp. 1974).	Doctor of medicine or osteopathy, resident, intern, school nurse.
Rhode Island	R.I. Gen. Laws Ann. §§40-11-1 to 40-11-10 (Supp. 1973).	1. Doctor of medicine, osteopath, resident, intern. 2. Any other person.
South Carolina	S.C. Code Ann. §§20-310 to 20-310-6 (Supp. 1973).	1. Practitioners of the healing arts. 2. Any other person.
South Dakota	S.D. Compiled Laws Ann. §§26-10-10 to 26-10-15 (1969), as amended, (Supp. 1974).	1. Physician, surgeon, dentist, osteopath, chiropractor, optometrist, podiatrist, psychologist, intern, resident, law enforcement officer, social worker.
Tennessee	Tenn. Code Ann. §§37-1201 to 37-1212 (Supp. 1974).	Any person.
Texas	Tex. Family Code Ann. §§34.01 to 34.06 (1973).	Any person.
Utah	Utah Code Ann. §§55-16-1 to 55-16-6 (1974).	Any person.
Vermont	Vt. Stat. Ann. §§1351 to 1355 (Supp. 1974).	Physician, surgeon, osteopath, chiropractor, resident, intern, physician's assistant, registered nurse, licensed practical nurse, medical examiner, dentist, police officer, psychologist, school teacher, principal, guidance counselor, social worker, probation officer, clergyman.
Virginia	Va. Code Ann. §§16.1-217.1 to 16.1-217.4 (Supp. 1974).	Any person licensed to practice medicine or any of the healing arts, any hospital resident or intern, any registered nurse, visiting nurse, public school nurse, registered social worker or associate social worker, probation officer, teacher in public and private schools.
Washington	Wash. Rev. Code §§26.44.010 to 26.44.080 (1972).	Chiropodist, chiropractor, dentist, osteopath, surgeon, doctor of medicine, Christian Science practitioner, professional school personnel (including, but not limited to, teachers, counselors, administrators, and school nurses), registered nurse, social worker, psychologist, pharmacist, clergyman, employee of Department of Social and Health Services.
West Virginia	W.Va. Code Ann. §§49-6A-1 to 49-6A-4 (1966), as amended, (Supp. 1974).	Physician, surgeon, resident, intern, doctor of healing arts, registered nurse, visiting nurse, school teacher, social worker.

Age Limit	Report to	Immunity Provision?	Physician-Patient Privilege Applicable?	Penalty?
18	County office of Department of Institutions, Social and Rehabilitative Services.	yes	yes	MISDEMEANOR.
15	Person in charge of institution, law enforcement agency.	yes	yes	MISDEMEANOR (§419.990).
18	Person in charge of institution, public child welfare agency.	yes	yes	SUMMARY OFFENSE; FINE NOT EXCEEDING $300; IN DEFAULT, IMPRISONMENT NOT EXCEEDING 90 DAYS.
18	Person in charge of institution, Department of Social and Rehabilitative Services, law enforcement agency.	yes	yes	
17	County department of public welfare, sheriff or law enforcement officer.	yes	yes	SENTENCE: 6 MO., $500, OR BOTH.
18	Person in charge of institution, judge of county court.	yes	yes	MISDEMEANOR. SENTENCE: 1 YEAR, $500, OR BOTH (§26-10-5).
18	Person in charge of institution, judge having juvenile jurisdiction of county, law enforcement agency.	yes	yes	MISDEMEANOR. SENTENCE: 3 MO., $50, OR BOTH.
18 (§11.01(1))	County Child Welfare Unit or county agency responsible for the protection of juvenile, any local or state law enforcement agency.	yes	yes	
Minor	Person in charge of institution, police, county sheriff, Division of Family Services.	yes	yes	MISDEMEANOR.
16	Person in charge of institution, commissioner of Social and Rehabilitative Services.	yes		FINE OF NOT MORE THAN $100.
16	Person in charge of institution, juvenile and domestic relations court, sheriff or chief of police.	Civil	yes	
18	Person in charge of institution, law enforcement agency, Department of Social and Health Services.	Civil	yes	MISDEMEANOR.
18	Person in charge of institution, Department of Welfare, prosecuting attorney.	yes		

State	Citation	Applies to
Wisconsin	Wis. Stat. Ann. §48.981 (Supp. 1974).	Physician, surgeon, nurse, hospital administrator, dentist, social worker, school administrator.
Wyoming	Wyo. Stat. Ann. §§14-28.7 to 14-28.13 (Supp. 1973).	1. Physician, surgeon, dentist, chiropractor, podiatrist, pharmacist, school teacher or administrator, social worker, osteopath, resident, intern, nurse, druggist, lab technician. 2. Any other person.
District of Columbia	D.C. Code Ann. §§2-161 to 2-166 (1973).	Physicians.

Age Limit	Report to	Immunity Provision?	Physician-Patient Privilege Applicable?	Penalty?
18 (§48.02)	County child welfare agency, sheriff, city police.	yes		SENTENCE: 6 MO., $100, OR BOTH.
18	Person in charge of institution; Department of Health and Social Services, Division of Public Assistance and Social Services.	yes	yes	
18	Person in charge of institution, police department.	yes	yes	

APPENDIX E

STATE-BY-STATE SUMMARY OF GOOD SAMARITAN LAWS

	A. Date of act or last amended act	B. Covers any emergency or accident	C. Covers only roadside accidents	D. Covers everyone	E. Covers in-state physicians	F. Covers out-of-state physicians	G. Covers in-state nurses	H. Covers out-of-state nurses	I. Does not cover acts of gross negligence or willful misconduct	J. Covers only gratuitous services
Alabama	1966	X			X	X	X	X	X	X
Alaska	1967	X		X					X	X
Arizona	1967	X		X	X	X	X	X	X	X
Arkansas	1963	X		X	X				X	X
California	1963	X			X		X		X	
Colorado	1965	X			X	X	X	X	X	
Connecticut	1969	X			X	X	X	X	X	X
Delaware	1963	X			X		X		X	
District of Columbia	1966	X			X	X	X	X	X	X
Florida	1965	X		X					X	X
Georgia	1963	X		X					X	X
Hawaii	1969	X		X					X	X
Idaho	1965	X		X					X	
Illinois	1970			X					X	X
Indiana	1964	X			X		X		X	X
Iowa	1970	X		X					X	X
Kansas	1969	X			X	X	X	X	X	X
Kentucky										
Louisiana	1964	X			X	X	X	X	X	X
Maine	1961	X			X		X		X	
Maryland	1973	X			X		X		X	X
Massachusetts	1970	X			X	X	X	X	X	X
Michigan	1964	X			X	X	X	X	X	
Minnesota	1971	X		X					X	
Mississippi	1964	X			X	X	X	X	X	
Missouri										
Montana	1963	X		X					X	X
Nebraska	1963	X			X	X	X	X	X	X
Nevada	1965	X		X					X	X
New Hampshire	1967	X			X	X	X	X	X	X
New Jersey	1968	X		X					X	
New Mexico	1963	X		X					X	X
New York	1968	X			X	X			X	X
North Carolina	1965		X	X					X	

STATE-BY-STATE SUMMARY OF GOOD SAMARITAN LAWS

	A. Date of act or last amended act	B. Covers any emergency or accident	C. Covers only roadside accidents	D. Covers everyone	E. Covers in-state physicians	F. Covers out-of-state physicians	G. Covers in-state nurses	H. Covers out-of-state nurses	I. Does not cover acts of gross negligence or willful misconduct	J. Covers only gratuitous services
North Dakota	1963	X			X	X			X	
Ohio	1964	X		X					X	X
Oklahoma	1969	X			X	X	X	X	X	
Oregon	1968	X			X	X	X	X	X	X
Pennsylvania	1965	X			X	X	X	X	X	
Rhode Island	1963	X			X	X			X	X
South Carolina	1964	X		X					X	X
South Dakota	1963	X			X	X	X	X	X	
Tennessee	1964	X		X					X	X
Texas	1964	X		X					X	X
Utah	1967	X			X		X		X	
Vermont	1967	X		X					X	X
Virginia	1968	X		X					X	X
Washington	1971	X			X				X	
West Virginia	1967	X		X					X	X
Wisconsin	1964	X			X		X		X	
Wyoming	1963	X		X					X	X

GLOSSARY OF LEGAL TERMS

Abortion: A termination of pregnancy or causing a miscarriage with intent to destroy the fetus.

Administrative agency: An arm of government which administers or carries out legislation; for example, Workmen's Compensation Commission.

Admissibility (of evidence): Worthiness of evidence that meets the legal rules of evidence and will be allowed to go to the jury.

Affidavit: A voluntary sworn statement of facts, or a voluntary declaration in writing of facts, that a person swears to be true before an official authorized to administer an oath.

Agency: The relationship in which one person acts for or represents another; for example, employer and employee.

Allegation: A statement that a person expects to be able to prove.

Appellant: The party who appeals the decision of a lower court to a court of higher jurisdiction.

Appellee: The party against whom an appeal to a higher court is taken.

Assault: An intentional act which is designed to make the victim fearful and which produces reasonable apprehension of harm.

Assignment: Transfer of rights or property.

Attestation: An indication by a witness that the documents of procedures required by law have been signed.

Battery: The touching of one person by another without permission.

Best evidence rule: A legal doctrine requiring that primary evidence of a fact (such as an original document) be introduced, or at least explained, before a copy can be introduced or testimony given concerning the fact.

Bona fide: In good faith; openly, honestly, or innocently; without knowledge or intent of fraud.

Borrowed servant: An employee temporarily under the control of another. The traditional example is that of a nurse employed by a hospital who is "borrowed" by a surgeon in the operating room. The temporary employer of the borrowed servant will be held responsible for the act of the borrowed servant under the doctrine of *respondeat superior*.

Civil law: The law of countries such as Germany and France which follow the Roman law system of jurisprudence in which all law is enacted. It is also the portion of American law which does not deal with crimes.

Closed shop contract: A labor-management agreement which provides that only members of a particular union may be hired.

Common law: The legal traditions of England and the United States where part of the law is developed by means of court decisions.

Concurring opinion: *See* Opinion of the court.

Confidential information: *See* Privileged communication.

Consent: A voluntary act by which one person agrees to allow someone else to do something. For medical liability purposes, consents should be in writing with an explanation of the procedures to be performed.

Coroner's jury: A special jury called by the coroner to determine whether the evidence concerning the cause of a death indicates that death was brought about by criminal means.

Counterclaim: A defendant's claim against a plaintiff.

Crime: An act against society in violation of the law. Crimes are prosecuted by and in the name of the state.

Criminal law: The division of the law dealing with crime and punishment.

Decedent: A deceased person.

Defamation: The injury of a person's reputation or character by willful and malicious statements made to a third person. Defamation includes both libel and slander.

Defendant: In a criminal case, the person accused of committing a crime. In a civil suit, the party against whom suit is brought demanding that he pay the other party legal relief.

Deposition: A sworn statement, made out of court, which may be admitted into evidence if it is impossible for a witness to attend in person.

Directed verdict: When a trial judge decides that the evidence or law is so clearly in favor of one party that it is pointless for the trial to proceed further, the judge directs the jury to return a verdict for that party.

Discovery: Pretrial activities of attorneys to determine what evidence the opposing side will present if the case comes to trial. Discovery prevents attorneys from being surprised during trial and facilitates out-of-court settlement.

Dissenting opinion: *See* Opinion of the court.

Emergency: A sudden unexpected occurrence or event causing a threat to life or health. The legal responsibilities of those involved in an emergency situation are measured according to the occurrence.

Employee: One who works for another in return for pay.

Employer: A person or firm that selects employees, pays their salaries or wages, retains the power of dismissal, and can control the employees' conduct during working hours.

Expert witness: One who has special training, experience, skill, and knowledge in a relevant area, and who is allowed to offer an opinion as testimony in court.

Federal question: Legal question involving the U.S. Constitution or a statute enacted by Congress.

Felony: A crime of a serious nature usually punishable by imprisonment for a period of longer than one year or by death.

Good samaritan law: A legal doctrine designed to protect those who stop to render aid in an emergency.

Grand jury: A jury called to determine whether there is sufficient evidence that a crime has been committed to justify bringing a case to trial. It is not the jury before which the case is tried to determine guilt or innocence.

Grand larceny: Theft of property valued at more than a specified amount (usually fifty dollars), thus constituting a felony instead of a misdemeanor.

Harm or injury: Any wrong or damage done to another, either to the person, to rights, or to property.

Hearsay rule: A rule of evidence that restricts the admissibility of evidence which is not the personal knowledge of the witness. Hearsay evidence is admissible only under strict rules.

Holographic will: A will handwritten by the testator.

In loco parentis: A legal doctrine that under certain circumstances the courts may assign a person to stand in the place of parents and possess their legal rights, duties, and responsibilities toward a child.

Independent contractor: One who agrees to undertake work without being under the direct control or direction of the employer.

Indictment: A formal written accusation of crime brought by a prosecuting attorney against one charged with criminal conduct.

Injunction: A court order requiring one to do or not to do a certain act.

Interrogatories: A list of questions sent from one party in a lawsuit to the other party to be answered.

Judge: An officer who guides court proceedings to ensure impartiality and enforce the rules of evidence. The trial judge determines the applicable law and states it to the jury. The appellate judge hears appeals and renders decisions concerning the correctness of actions of the trial judge, the law of the case, and the sufficiency of the evidence.

Jurisprudence: The philosophy or science of law upon which a particular legal system is built.

Jury: A certain number of persons selected and sworn to hear the evidence and determine the facts in a case.

Larceny: Taking another person's property without consent with the intent to deprive the owner of its use and ownership.

Liability: An obligation one has incurred or might incur through any act or failure to act.

Liability insurance: A contract to have someone else pay for any liability or loss thereby in return for the payment of premiums.

Libel: A false or malicious writing that is intended to defame or dishonor another person and is published so that someone besides the one defamed will observe it

License: A permit from the state allowing certain acts to be performed, usually for a specific period of time.

Litigation: A trial in court to determine legal issues, rights, and duties between the parties to the litigation.

Malpractice: Professional misconduct, improper discharge of professional duties, or failure to meet the standard of care of a professional which resulted in harm to another.

Mayhem: The crime of intentionally disfiguring or dismembering another.

Misdemeanor: An unlawful act of a less serious nature than a felony, usually punishable by fine or imprisonment for a term of less than one year.

Negligence: Carelessness, failure to act as an ordinary prudent person, or action contrary to what a reasonable person would have done.

Next of kin: Those persons who by the law of descent would be adjudged the closest blood relatives of the decedent.

Non compos mentis: "Not of sound mind"; suffering from some form of mental defect.

Notary public: A public official who administers oaths and certifies the validity of documents.

Nuncupative will: Oral statement intended as a last will made in anticipation of death.

Opinion of the court: In an appellate court decision, the reasons for the decision. One judge writes the opinion for the majority of the court. Judges who agree with the result but for different reasons may write concurring opinions explaining their reasons. Judges who disagree with the majority may write dissenting opinions.

Ordinance: A law passed by a municipal legislative body.

Perjury: The willful act of giving false testimony under oath.

Petit larceny: Theft of property usually valued below fifty dollars and classed as a misdemeanor.

Plaintiff: The party to a civil suit who brings the suit seeking damages or other legal relief.

Police power: The power of the state to protect the health, safety, morals, and general welfare of the people.

Privileged communication: Statement made to an attorney, physician, spouse, or anyone else in a position of trust. Because of the confidential nature of such information, the law protects it from being revealed, even in court. The term is applied in two distinct situations. First, the communications between certain persons, such as physician and patient, cannot be divulged without consent of the patient. Second, in some situations the law provides an exemption from liability for disclosing information where there is a higher duty to speak, such as statutory reporting requirements.

Probabe: The judicial proceeding which determines the existence and validity of a will.

Probate Court: Court with jurisdiction over wills. Its powers range from deciding the validity of a will to distributing property.

Proximate: In immediate relation with something else. In negligence cases, the careless act must be the proximate cause of injury.

Real evidence: Evidence furnished by tangible things, such as weapons, bullets, and equipment.

Rebuttal: The giving of evidence to contradict the effect of evidence introduced by the opposing party.

Regulatory agency: An arm of the government which enforces legislation regulating an act or activity in a particular area; for example, the Federal Food and Drug Administration.

Release: A statement signed by one person relinquishing a right or claim against another person, usually for a valuable consideration.

Res gestae: All of the surrounding events which become part of an incident. If statements are made as part of the incident they are admissible in court as *res gestae,* in spite of the hearsay rule.

Res ipsa loquitur: "The thing speaks for itself." A doctrine of law applicable to cases where the defendant had exclusive control of the thing which caused the harm and where the harm ordinarily could not have occurred without negligent conduct.

Respondeat superior: "Let the master answer." The employer is responsible for the legal consequences of the acts of the servant or employee while acting within the scope of employment.

Shop book rule: If books are kept in the usual course of business they may be introduced in court so long as they are properly authenticated and held in proper custody.

Slander: An oral statement made with intent to dishonor or defame another person when made in the presence of a third person.

Standard of care: Those acts performed or omitted that an ordinary prudent person would have performed or omitted. It is a measure against which a defendant's conduct is compared.

Stare decisis: "Let the decision stand." The legal principle indicating that courts should apply previous decisions to subsequent cases involving similar facts and questions.

State statute; statutory law: A declaration of the legislative branch of government having the force of law.

Statute of limitations: A legal limit on the time allowed for filing suit in civil matters, usually measured from the time of the wrong or from the time when a reasonable man would have discovered the wrong.

Subpoena: A court order requiring one to appear in court to give testimony.

Subpoena duces tecum: A subpoena that commands a person to come to court and to produce whatever documents are named in the order.

Subrogation: Substitution of one person for another in reference to a lawful claim or right.

Suit: Court proceeding where one person seeks damages or other legal remedies from another. The term is not usually used in criminal cases.

Summons: A court order directed to the sheriff to notify the defendant in a civil suit that a suit has been filed and when and where to appear.

Testimony: Oral statement of a witness given under oath at a trial.

Torte: A civil wrong. Torts may be intentional or unintentional.

Tortfeasor: One who commits a tort.

Trial court: The court in which evidence is presented to a judge or jury for decision.

Uniform act: A model act concerning a particular area of the law created by a nonlegal body in the hope that it will be enacted in all states to achieve uniformity in that area of the law.

Union shop contract: A labor-management agreement making continued employment contingent upon joining the union.

Verdict: The formal declaration of a jury's findings of fact, signed by the jury foreman and presented to the court.

Waiver: The intentional giving up of a right, such as allowing another person to testify to information that would ordinarily be protected as a privileged communication.

Will: A legal declaration of the intentions a person wishes to have carried out after death concerning property, children, or estate.

Witness: One who is called to give testimony in a court of law.

Written authorization: Consent given in writing specifically empowering someone to do something.

INDICES

INDEX OF CASES

INDEX OF TOPICS